The Kubrick Legacy

The six chapters assembled in *The Kubrick Legacy* showcase important trends in the evolution of filmmaker Stanley Kubrick's artistic legacy.
 In the 20 years since his death an enormous range of information and scholarship has surfaced, in part from the Kubrick estate's public preservation, archiving, exhibition and promulgation of the auteur's staggering collection of research materials and film artifacts. These essays from international scholars chart incarnations of the official Kubrick exhibition of extensive artifacts touring the globe for the past decade; the filmmaker's lasting impact on established authors with whom he collaborated; the profound influence of Kubrick's use of existing music in film scores; the exponential rise of conspiracy theories and (mis)interpretation of his work since his death; the repeated imitation of and homage to his oeuvre across decades of international television advertising; and the (re)discovery of Kubrick on screen in both documentary form and dramatic characterization.
 The Kubrick Legacy provides a tantalizing, critical snapshot of the enduring impact and influence of one of the twentieth century's most enigmatic and consummate screen artists.

Mick Broderick is Associate Professor of Media Analysis at Murdoch University, Australia. His major publications include *Reconstructing Strangelove* (2017), editions of the reference work *Nuclear Movies* (1988, 1991), and as editor or co-editor, *Hibakusha Cinema* (1996, 1999, 2014), *Interrogating Trauma* (2010) and *Trauma, Media, Art* (2011). He is currently completing two co-authored monographs: *Trauma and Disability in Mad Max: Beyond the Road Warrior's Fury* (with Katie Ellis) and *Virtual Realities: Case Studies in Immersion, Aesthetics and Affect* (with Stuart Bender), both for release in 2019.

The Kubrick Legacy

Edited by Mick Broderick

LONDON AND NEW YORK

First published 2019
by Routledge
2 Park Square, Milton Park, Abingdon, Oxon OX14 4RN

and by Routledge
52 Vanderbilt Avenue, New York, NY 10017

Routledge is an imprint of the Taylor & Francis Group, an informa business

© 2019 selection and editorial matter, Mick Broderick; individual chapters, the contributors

The right of Mick Broderick to be identified as the author of the editorial material, and of the authors for their individual chapters, has been asserted in accordance with sections 77 and 78 of the Copyright, Designs and Patents Act 1988.

All rights reserved. No part of this book may be reprinted or reproduced or utilised in any form or by any electronic, mechanical, or other means, now known or hereafter invented, including photocopying and recording, or in any information storage or retrieval system, without permission in writing from the publishers.

Trademark notice: Product or corporate names may be trademarks or registered trademarks, and are used only for identification and explanation without intent to infringe.

British Library Cataloguing-in-Publication Data
A catalogue record for this book is available from the British Library

Library of Congress Cataloging-in-Publication Data
Names: Broderick, Mick, editor.
Title: The Kubrick legacy / edited by Mick Broderick.
Description: London ; New York : Routledge, 2019. | Includes bibliographical references and index.
Identifiers: LCCN 2018056634 (print) | LCCN 2018059584 (ebook) | ISBN 9780429059728 (ebook) | ISBN 9780367181420 | ISBN 9780367181420 (hardback : alk.paper) | ISBN 9780429059728 (ebk)
Subjects: LCSH: Kubrick, Stanley—Criticism and interpretation.
Classification: LCC PN1998.3.K83 (ebook) | LCC PN1998.3.K83 K835 2019 (print) | DDC 791.4302/33092—dc23
LC record available at https://lccn.loc.gov/2018056634

ISBN: 978-0-367-18142-0 (hbk)
ISBN: 978-0-429-05972-8 (ebk)

Typeset in Times New Roman
by Apex CoVantage, LLC

For Katharina

Contents

List of contributors ix
Acknowledgments xi

1 The Kubrick legacy: an introduction 1
   MICK BRODERICK

2 Kubrick and curation: inside TIFF's *Stanley Kubrick: the exhibition* 7
   DRU JEFFRIES

3 The rise of Doctor Strangelove: Stanley Kubrick, Peter George, Herman Kahn, and a new world morality 22
   GRAHAM ALLEN

4 Looking back, looking ahead: Kubrick and music 37
   CHRISTINE GENGARO

5 Dramatizing Kubrick: *Room 237* and other conspiracies 52
   MANCA PERKO

6 Kubrick: tropes in advertising 67
   JAMES MARINACCIO

7 Kubrick on screen 88
   MICK BRODERICK

8	**Conclusion** MICK BRODERICK	106
	Index	109

Contributors

Graham Allen is a professor in the School of English, University College Cork. His publications include *Harold Bloom: A Poetics of Conflict* (1994), *Intertextuality* (2000: 2nd Ed. 2011), and *Roland Barthes* (2003). His latest poetry collection, *The Madhouse System*, was published in 2016.

Mick Broderick is Associate Professor of Media Analysis at Murdoch University. His major publications include *Reconstructing Strangelove* (2017), editions of the reference work *Nuclear Movies* (1988, 1991) and as editor or co-editor, *Hibakusha Cinema* (1996, 1999, 2014), *Interrogating Trauma* (2010), and *Trauma, Media, Art: New Perspectives* (2011). He is currently completing two co-authored monographs: *Trauma and Disability in Mad Max: Beyond the Road Warrior's Fury* (with Katie Ellis) and *Virtual Realities: Case Studies in Immersion, Aesthetics and Affect* (with Stuart Bender), both for release in 2019.

Christine Gengaro teaches music history, music theory, and voice at Los Angeles City College. She received her Ph.D. in historical musicology from the University of Southern California in 2005 and her published articles on film music and classical music in media appear in numerous journals and books. Her book *Listening to Stanley Kubrick: the Music in His Films* was published in 2013 and her *Experiencing: Chopin* was released in December of 2017. She is currently editing a new edition of *This Man and Music* by Anthony Burgess.

Dru Jeffries is the author of Comic Book Film Style (University of Texas Press, 2017) and the editor of #WWE: Professional Wrestling in the Digital Age (Indiana University Press, 2019). He teaches in the Cultural Studies department at Wilfrid Laurier University.

x *Contributors*

James Marinaccio lives in Orlando, Florida, works in magazine publishing and is an occasional freelance writer. He has assisted authors, web designers, and filmmakers in various Kubrick projects. He was instrumental in having Stanley Kubrick inducted into the Bronx Walk of Fame in 2001. He is currently the administrator of the Facebook group The Stanley Kubrick Appreciation Society and assists with the production of the Kubrick's Universe Podcast. From 2001 to 2004 he worked at *Ad Age Magazine, Creativity Magazine*, Adcritic.com, and *Madison & Vine* newsletter.

Manca Perko is a Ph.D. student at the University of East Anglia in Norwich, UK, completing research on Kubrick's filmmaking practice in relation to creative autonomy and collaborative authorship. She is also a film practitioner.

Acknowledgments

My sincere gratitude is extended to the authors assembled here both for their wonderful perspectives on the Kubrick legacy and for their ongoing commitment to this project, despite unexpected delays and some tardiness on my part. I hope this volume will garner further interest in their individual Kubrick scholarship and I thank them all for their patience and perseverance. Thanks also to my anonymous peer reviewers for their incisive comments and germane suggestions. For the editorial and production stewardship, Natalie Foster and Jennifer Vennall at Routledge have been exemplary, as have Autumn Spalding and Denise File at Apex CoAdvantage.

In recent years I have greatly benefited from the knowledge, insight, and acumen of Katharina Kubrick, Tony Frewin, and Richard Daniels on many matters Kubrick, as well as from several contributors and interlocutors at The Stanley Kubrick Appreciation Society, A.M.K., and The Kubrick Site. My thanks to all.

Finally, to Christine Spiegel . . . merci, mon amour.

1 The Kubrick legacy
An introduction

Mick Broderick

2018 was an auspicious year for the Kubrick legacy and one that bodes well for the future. Commemorating the 50th anniversary of the release of *2001: A Space Odyssey* (1968), the past 12 months have witnessed multiple events and celebrations, alongside other cultural and artistic manifestations, to honor Kubrick's landmark production. In May of that year filmmaker Christopher Nolan presented an analogue, "unrestored" 70mm print of the movie during the Cannes Film Festival and has promoted its exhibition at select U.S. theaters still equipped with 70mm projectors (Sopan 2018). In the U.K. a set of commemorative stamps were stuck by the Isle of Man post office to honor the movie's production and release. Showcasing key artifacts from the Kubrick estate, the Deutsches Filmmuseum in Frankfurt presented *Kubrick's 2001: 50 Years A Space Odyssey* exhibition. Reprising a previous Los Angeles exhibition, British artist Simon Birch installed his large immersive work "The Barmecide Feast" at the Smithsonian's Air and Space Museum as the centerpiece of a display celebrating the anniversary of *2001*'s release. The massive artwork reconstructs the faux Louis XIV-era bedroom that houses David Bowman's rapid evolutionary transformation at the conclusion of *2001*.[1]

The vast 1,000m² official Stanley Kubrick traveling exhibition continues to roll out across the globe with shows in Copenhagen and Mexico City during 2017, and next on display in Barcelona from October 2018 to March 2019 and London from April to September 2019 (Deutsches Filmmuseum 2018). Since it premiered in Germany in 2004, to date, well over a million attendees have visited the exhibit in Europe, Australia, Central America, Asia, North America, and South America.

Corresponding with this public outreach of artifacts and memorabilia, a number of key publications on the film and Kubrick's other artistry have appeared this anniversary year. Michael Benson's adroit and comprehensive history, *Space Odyssey: Stanley Kubrick, Arthur C. Clarke, and the Making of a Masterpiece* (Simon & Schuster), and James Fenwick's scholarly collection *Understanding Kubrick's 2001: A Space Odyssey* (Intellect), provide fascinating and compelling insights into the filmmaker and his creative approach. Anthony Frewin's compendium of *2001*'s excised prologue, *Are We Alone: The Stanley Kubrick Extraterrestrial-Intelligence Interviews* (Ashgrove), is fortunately now back in print with an updated introduction. There's even an adult coloring book: *Stanley Kubrick Universe Inspired Coloring Book: The Greatest and the Most Influential Director, 2001: A Space Odyssey and Dr. Strangelove Mastermind* (CreateSpace).

Other recently published contributions to the burgeoning field of Kubrick studies range from Nathan Abrams's deeply researched study, *Stanley Kubrick: New York Jewish Intellectual* (Rutgers U.P.), and self-published fan appraisals such as Todd Alcott's marginal *Kubrick: Five Films: an Analysis* (2018), through to Luc Sante's largely pictorial book *Stanley Kubrick Photographs: Through a Different Lens* (Taschen America). The latter further renews interest in the filmmaker's pre-cinematic visual work as a staff photographer for *Look* magazine and serves to catalogue the recent exhibition of Kubrick's pictures at the Museum of the City of New York (Lang 2018; MTCNY 2018).

The past few years have been equally fecund, demonstrating that Kubrick's legacy remains ripe for research and scholarship, including books by principal (new history) Kubrick scholar Peter Krämer on *Dr. Strangelove*, among others; the art publisher Black Books' collection of essays edited by Krämer, Tatjana Ljujic, and Richard Daniels, *Stanley Kubrick: New Perspectives*, largely informed by holdings at the Stanley Kubrick Archive; my own revisionist archival history, *Reconstructing Strangelove*; and the informative and sometimes moving (auto)biography *Stanley Kubrick and Me: Thirty Years at His Side* by one of Kubrick's trusted assistants, Emilio D'Alessandro (with Filippo Ulivieri). The latter book inspired the documentary *S is for Stanley* (Dir: Alex Infascelli, 2015) featuring D'Alessandro. A similar biographical documentary, *Filmworker* (Dir: Tony Zierra 2018), highlighted the vicissitudes of Leon Vitali, long-time Kubrick assistant, collaborator, and *Barry Lyndon* actor (Lord Bullingdon). Kubrick's legacy can thus be understood as additionally influencing and impacting his contemporary worker-collaborators (and their loved ones) in both demanding and stimulating ways. One wonders when other staunch and steadfast Kubrick aides—such as Anthony Frewin, Margaret Adams, and Andros Epaminondas—will have their significant contributions similarly heralded.

Evidence of the Kubrick legacy also includes regular live performances of the classical music used to accompany screenings of *2001* and *Barry Lyndon*. Memorabilia from the filmmaker's productions is in constant demand via online auctions, such as those on eBay, where at any given time a search on "Kubrick" will reveal tens of thousands of items—from authentic studio marketing materials (stills, lobbycards, posters, press kits) and their reproduction, to many thousands of fan-based artworks, including t-shirts, socks and jackets displaying motifs, phrases or key images from every film, and portraits of the director himself. Other eBay items replicate props with great precision, including masks for sale in 2018 by a Venetian craftsman, duplicating those worn in *Eyes Wide Shut*.

Premium Kubrick memorabilia occasionally features at Sotheby's auctions. In July 2017 a hand-corrected set of page proofs for the heavily illustrated *Stanley Kubrick's A Clockwork Orange: Based on the Novel by Anthony Burgess* (New York: Ballantine Books) fetched £9,000 at nearly twice the estimate.[2] A single 8 ¾ × 8 ¼ inch (22.2 × 21 cm) black and white ferrotyped photo titled "Mickey, the Shoeshine Boy," taken by Kubrick for *Look* magazine, was sold in April 2010 by Sotheby's for US$18,750. Five letters from Kubrick to the Boulting Brothers, written during the preproduction of *Dr. Strangelove*, were recently sold for £1,875 by Bonhams auctioneers.

The Kubrick legacy also abounds via global fandom, especially with the advent of social media and crowd-sourced research to complement existing websites dedicated to the memory of the filmmaker and his oeuvre. Such enthusiasm almost daily unearths gems of detail and information, often 'correcting' or re-interpreting existing orthodoxies. One such example is the recent upload and circulation of a previously unknown interview for Japanese television from 1980, where Kubrick's voice over the telephone is recorded, on camera, answering questions about the "meaning" of the ending of *2001* and *The Shining*, something the writer-director-producer assiduously refused to summarize or otherwise interpret in public for decades (Yaoi 1980).

Tapping into this reappraisal and renaissance, *The Kubrick Legacy* is a modest attempt to showcase a variety of scholarly approaches to the lasting cultural resonances of the renowned filmmaker. As such, it deliberately seeks to complement and advance my 2017 edited dossier "Post-Kubrick" (Broderick 2017), drawn from a range of papers delivered at the 2016 *Stanley Kubrick: Cult Auteur* conference and exhibition in Leicester—a lively gathering that has spawned subsequent collections (Fenwick, Hunter, and Pezzotta 2017a, 2017b).

The six essays collected here each present representative samples of the Kubrick legacy as discreet case studies. Naturally, these examples are the proverbial tip of the iceberg. Future work will be better paced to provide more comprehensive evaluations as to Kubrick's intellectual, emotional, industrial, and artistic endowment. The contribution by **Dru Jeffries**, "Kubrick and curation: inside TIFF's *Stanley Kubrick: the exhibition*," cogently interrogates how the processes of curation and organization involved in the Toronto

4 *Mick Broderick*

International Film Festival's (TIFF) staging of the Kubrick estate-sanctioned exhibition contribute to the management of the filmmaker's official legacy. Deploying interviews with TIFF staff and careful analysis of the exhibition itself, Jeffries explores how Stanley Kubrick is represented as a curatorial 'presence' throughout the exhibition. The author demonstrates how the TIFF exhibition (especially in combination with its gift shop) embodies a larger trend within film culture whereby auteurs are increasingly understood through paratexts, both official and fan-made, that can circulate more freely than films.

Kubrick's influence on the writers who worked in collaboration with him is exemplified in **Graham Allen**'s "The rise of Doctor Strangelove: Stanley Kubrick, Peter George, Herman Kahn, and a New World morality." Allen maintains that one of the purposes of studying adaptation is to allow, periodically, for a reassessment of the dominant assumptions concerning the relation between films and their non-filmic, largely literary, intertexts. The essay considers the impact of Peter George's intense collaboration with Kubrick on *Dr. Strangelove* and the writer's follow-up, post-holocaust novel, *Commander-1*, explicitly dedicated to Kubrick, and crafted specifically as an historical response to the rapidly evolving global nuclear threat.

In "Looking back, looking ahead: Kubrick and music," **Christine Gengaro** considers the ways in which Kubrick's musical choices have influenced other filmmakers (e.g. Terrence Malick as an obvious 'inheritor') and the greater role Kubrick's style and choices have played in the manner films are scored post-*2001: A Space Odyssey*. According to Gengaro, studying Kubrick's films makes one aware of pre-existent music in film scores across film history, and she skillfully demonstrates that Kubrick is a major part of this legacy, asserting there is perhaps no other director so responsible for such a significant shift in film *scoring* techniques.

One curious and confounding legacy of Kubrick's films, and his mutable public persona, is the perpetuation of spurious claims surrounding his life and artistic praxis. In "Dramatizing Kubrick: *Room 237* and other conspiracies," **Manca Perko** examines the phenomenon by studying some of the more extreme readings of Kubrick's *The Shining* (1980), as presented in Rodney Ascher's documentary *Room 237* (2012) and other 'conspiracy' theories circulating in popular culture, such as YouTube videos of Kubrick's alleged 'confession' to filming the moon landing, and in-depth explanations of it as seen in *Dark Side of the Moon: Stanley Kubrick and the Fake Moon Landings* (2014). Perko argues that these dubious representations and evaluations of screen art in popular culture affect readings, not only of Kubrick's films, but the wider perception of his legacy in social and cultural contexts.

Traditional television advertising has arguably been the most influential and possibly invasive form of audio-visual exposure in Western culture. **James Marinaccio**'s chapter, "Kubrick: tropes in advertising," pivots to those commercials (over 100) from the early 1980s onwards that draw from

Stanley Kubrick's oeuvre. Marinaccio identifies aspects of Kubrickian homage (or influence) in TV advertising, especially *2001* and *The Shining*, while noting creative gestures towards *Spartacus*, *Lolita*, *Eyes Wide Shut*, *Dr. Strangelove*, *Full Metal Jacket* and *Clockwork Orange*. The chapter further notes, typologically, that several advertisements present *multiple* expressions of Kubrick's films in a single commercial.

Finally, **my own essay**, "Kubrick on screen," examines the evolution of the filmmaker's public mythology and its alignment with his few official screen appearances, in newsreels and behind-the-scenes videos as conscious acts of public documentation, as opposed to his absent-presence in "non-fiction" screen works such *Stanley Kubrick: A Life in Pictures* (2001), and *Stanley Kubrick's Boxes* (2008). I also contrast the quasi-fictional, dramatic representations of Kubrick as a screen character and chart their changing artistic rendering. These include actors Peter Coyote in the low-budget production *Stranger's Kiss* (1983); John Malkovich as Kubrick-impersonator, Alan Conway, in *Color Me Kubrick* (2005); Stanley Tucci as the director opposite Geoffrey Rush in *The Life and Death of Peter Sellers* (2008); alongside evocations in the post-millennial conspiracy-comedies, *Moonwalkers* (2015) and *Operation Avalanche* (2016).

Notes

1 Despite some commentators arguing about the precise art period of the room, Kubrick noted that the space was essentially an extraterrestrial "human zoo," inaccurately rendered. In a 1980 interview for Japanese television, Kubrick reluctantly described the scene: "the idea was supposed to be that he is taken in by godlike entities; creatures of pure, er, energy and intelligence with no shape or form and they put him in what I suppose you could describe as a human zoo, to study him. He spends his whole life from that point on in that room, and he has no sense of time, it just seems to happen, as it does in the film. And they choose this room, which is a very inaccurate replica of French architecture, deliberately so. Inaccurate because one was suggesting that they had some idea of something that he might think was pretty but weren't quite sure, just as we aren't quite sure about what to do in zoos with animals, to give them what we think is their natural environment" (Kubrick 1980/2018).
2 An earlier auction in 2008 for Kubrick's extensively hand-written revisions to Jeremy Bernstein's 1966 *New Yorker* article "How about a little game" was not sold (estimate: US$5–7,000). See: www.sothebys.com/en/auctions/ecatalogue/ 2008/fine-books-and-manuscripts-including-americana-n08501/lot.185. html?locale=en

Works cited

Broderick, Mick. 2017. "Post-Kubrick: On the Filmmaker's Influence and Legacy." Post-Kubrick Dossier. *Screening the Past*, no. 42. www.screeningthepast. com/2017/09/post-kubrick-on-the-filmmakers-influence-and-legacy/.

Deutsches Filmmuseum. 2018. "Stanley Kubrick: Exhibition Tour." www.stanleykubrick.de/en/ausstellungstour-exhibition-on-tour/.
Fenwick, J., I. Q. Hunter, and E. Pezzotta. 2017a. "The Stanley Kubrick Archive: A Dossier of New Research: Introduction." *Historical Journal of Film, Radio and Television* 37, no. 3: 367–72.
———. 2017b. "Stanley Kubrick: A Retrospective. Introduction." *Cinergie*, no. 12. https://cinergie.unibo.it/article/view/7341/7291.
Kubrick, Stanley. 1980/2018. "Interview Transcript Between Jun'ichi Yao and Stanley Kubrick." Transcribed by Rod Munday. *The Kubrick Site*. www.visual-memory.co.uk/amk/doc/0122.html.
Lang, Brent. 2018. "Stanley Kubrick's Stunning Early Photographs on Display at Museum of the City of New York." *Variety*, April 2. https://variety.com/2018/film/news/stanley-kubrick-museum-of-the-city-of-new-york-photos-1202741533/.
MTCNY. 2018. "Through a Different Lens: Stanley Kubrick Photographs." May 1. www.youtube.com/watch?v=otJ6VCS4abw.
Sopan, Deb. 2018. "Christopher Nolan's Version of Vinyl: Unrestoring '2001.'" *New York Times*, May 11. www.nytimes.com/2018/05/11/movies/2001-a-space-odyssey-christopher-nolan-cannes.html.
Sothebys. 2017. "Corrected Page Proofs of 'Stanley Kubrick's a Clockwork Orange: Based on the Novel by Anthony Burgess.'" July 11. www.sothebys.com/en/auctions/ecatalogue/2017/english-literature-l17404/lot.163.html.
Yaoi, Jun'ichi. 1980. "The Shining—Unseen Interviews with Stanley Kubrick & Vivian Kubrick, 1980 (Jun'ichi Yaoi/矢追 純一)." www.youtube.com/watch?v=fVlXbS0SNqk.

2 Kubrick and curation

Inside TIFF's *Stanley Kubrick: the exhibition*

Dru Jeffries

In an essay about Virginia Woolf's house museum, Nuala Hancock (2010, 119) writes that "Death and the passage of time give us license to transgress accepted inter-subjective boundaries; to 'break into' another's life; to handle, to investigate, to appropriate their private things. Such privileged encounters bring us into closer contact with the other; render the intangible tangible." Few film directors were as intangible—as inscrutable, as inaccessible—during their lives as Stanley Kubrick; tellingly, Vincent LoBrutto's *Stanley Kubrick: A Biography* opens with a prologue entitled "The Myth of the Reclusive Auteur," in which he describes how Kubrick's reluctance to enter the spotlight resulted in "a torrent of apocryphal stories [that produced] a mythology more than a man" (1997, 1). As Hancock's description of Woolf's house museum suggests, however, Kubrick's death held the potential for greater and more direct access to the unknowable auteur than had previously been possible.

Predictably, the donation of the director's personal archive to the University of the Arts London in 2007 has had a paradigm-shifting effect on Kubrick studies, providing scholars with primary resources that had previously been stashed away in boxes scattered across the director's estate. Now that the contents of these boxes are accessible, Kubrick scholarship has moved from a discourse primarily oriented around textual analysis to one based more on archival research. By looking through this collection of physical objects, researchers seek to understand not just Kubrick's films, but also the man himself. This is in line with the shift in auteur studies that Dana Polan (2001) observed in his article "Auteur Desire":

> where classic auteurism relied on intuitions about the ways in which the director works to author a film and posited above all that personal artistic expression emerged in mysterious ways from ineffable deep wells of creativity, new advances in historiography (for example, the potentials that gritty archival work offers) have led, in contrast, to a

greater concreteness and detail in the examination of just what the work of the director involves. [...] Creativity now comes from concrete (and therefore, analyzable) patient application of rules and conventions [...] rather than ineffable genius.

Those who want to demystify Kubrick and his "ineffable genius" can now do so through such "gritty archival work." Indeed, if the Archive does one thing, it is to reify Kubrick's creative process: his perfectionism, his penchant for research, and his need to collect and catalogue objects and information alike are made manifest in the seemingly endless collection of documents and ephemera preserved in the Stanley Kubrick Archive (hereafter SKA). Recent scholarship has drawn heavily on these resources, promising "to offer new perspectives on the filmmaker and his films" (Ljujić 2015, 15).

While the influence of the SKA can hardly be overstated in terms of its impact on scholarship, access is nevertheless restricted to researchers local to London or those with considerable research and travel allowances. Between 2007 and 2016, 13,910 people visited the Archives and Special Collections Centre at University of the Arts London; in the 2015–2016 school year alone, the Center had 1,816 visits, approximately 80% of which (~1,453) consulted Kubrick-related material.[1] By comparison, the Los Angeles mounting of the Kubrick exhibition received a whopping 243,792 visitors—a daily average of more than 1,000 individuals—over its 242-day run (Ng 2013), and the travelling exhibition as a whole has welcomed "well over a million visitors" and counting (Broderick 2017). As these figures indicate, exponentially more people will encounter archival materials through the touring museum exhibition than the SKA. Beginning with its inaugural installation at Frankfurt's Deutsche Filmmuseum in 2004, the Kubrick exhibition has traveled to 17 cities around the world, including Melbourne, Paris, Kraków, and Seoul, to name just a few. As the original curator Hans-Peter Reichmann (2014, 10) writes in the exhibition's catalogue, the SKA "does not betray a systematical order, process of selection, or a will to interpretation." When assembling an exhibition, it therefore falls to the curator to function as "a culling figure" (Balzer 2014, Kindle loc. 621), tasked not only with cherry-picking a small portion of the available archival materials for display—thereby conferring special value and historical significance upon them—but also with exhibiting these artifacts to the public in a controlled and deliberate way. While the materials that constitute the exhibition differ little from location to location, the ways in which they are organized and displayed can vary a great deal based on the intentions and intuitions of each new site's curator(s), as well as the affordances or limitations of the specific exhibition space; as a result, each mounting of the exhibition creates new contexts for these objects, thereby constructing a unique narrative. As such, it's necessary to consider each exhibition as a text in its own right. This essay will focus specifically on the exhibition's 12th stop, at the TIFF Bell Lightbox in Toronto, Ontario, Canada (October 31, 2014–January 25, 2015). By analyzing TIFF's approach to design and curation in *Stanley Kubrick: The Exhibition* (hereafter *SK:TE*), I hope to illuminate some of the ways in which Kubrick's legacy is actively being shaped in the present, in this case some 15 years after his death.

Exhibition as medium, curator as author

While the touring exhibition may seem to place visitors in the unmediated presence of Kubrick's ephemera, it is in fact a mediating force insofar as it cannot transmit information neutrally: by "positioning and controlling [...] the spectator in a space of display" (O'Neill 2012, 90), curators influence visitors' experiences and their potential interpretations of an exhibition's content. This extends to the aesthetic design of the gallery space; as art dealer and curator Seth Siegelaub (2014, 36) asserts, every curatorial choice made "in the predetermination of the exhibition" has the potential to "hinder the viewing of the intrinsic value of each work of art" or artifact on display. If each object within an exhibition is considered as an individual text in its own right, then the context provided by curators can usefully be considered as paratextual in nature, inevitably affecting each viewer's experience and interpretation of a given text. As Jonathan Gray (2010, Kindle loc. 560) writes, "Each paratext acts like an airlock to acclimatize us to a certain text, and it demands or suggests certain reading strategies." When such framing devices become attractions in their own right, there is a very real danger that the ostensible content of the exhibition—the works of art or artifacts on display—may be overshadowed by what we might playfully call *curatorial exhibitionism*. Conceptual artist Daniel Buren (2014, 43) has concluded, perhaps a bit bitterly, that "The subject of exhibitions tends more and more to be not so much the exhibition of *works of art*, as the exhibition of the *exhibition as a work of art*" (emphases mine). By thus directing visitors' attention and interpretative energies from the trees to the forest, if you will, the curator can supplant the artist(s) whose work is on display, with the theme or narrative meaning of the exhibition itself outweighing any individual piece of art in importance; in such cases, the significance of individual works is based primarily on the contribution each makes to the *curator's* vision. Paul O'Neill (2012, 5) has dubbed this phenomenon the "curator-as-auteur": "the curated exhibition [provides] a distinct style and method of self-presentation [in which] *curators* [construct] subjective 'new truths' about art, often presented as universal narratives within an overarching curatorial frame" (emphasis mine). With regard to TIFF's *SK:TE* we must remain mindful of the ways in which the meaning or significance of the archival materials on display may be "predetermined" by the mediating function of the exhibition itself, and in particular how the arrangement and juxtaposition of these objects may service a particular curatorial narrative or theory. It's also worth flagging the ways in which *SK:TE* is distinct from the kinds of exhibitions being discussed in the above quotations. According to Lucy Steeds (2014, 13), studying exhibitions "means prioritizing [the work of art's] becoming public—its moment of meeting a public or, rather, plural publics." This is obviously one area in which the Kubrick exhibition differs from the typical contemporary art exhibition: first, it is expected that *SK:TE*'s visitors would be somewhat familiar with some of Kubrick's films prior to entering the exhibition; second, the works of art being celebrated are absent from the exhibition itself.[2] While Jihoon Kim (2017, 470) conceptualizes the Kubrick exhibition in terms of the art museum's "white cube," I would argue that *SK:TE* is more accurately characterized as an exhibition of historical artifacts that purports to present a narrative of historical or scientific truth, such as we might find in a natural history or science museum. If *SK:TE* marks the "becoming public" of anything, it is of foretexts, paratexts, and certain constituent components of Kubrick's films (e.g., props, costumes). *SK:TE* favors what Christopher Whitehead (2012, 37) has referred to as a "process-based" approach, compared to the more common "product-based" approach in which only the completed work is displayed. In a way, *SK:TE* marks the becoming public of Kubrick himself, or at least his creative process as an artist, as reconstituted and reified by a curated selection of archival materials. Though the public doesn't confront the works of art themselves, *SK:TE* still functions as art exhibitions tend to—that is, as an "occasion when [. . .] meaning and import are collectively debated" (Steeds 2014, 13) and as an opportunity for visitors to enrich their appreciation or understanding of an artist.

Finally, *SK:TE*'s status as part of a touring exhibition warrants mention. David Balzer (2014, Kindle loc. 1223) describes touring exhibitions as "cost-cutting initiatives, part of the audience-oriented museum shift of the 1990s [. . .] They are also, often, populist and an easier draw; the same phenomenon is occurring in the theatre world, with endlessly touring productions of major Broadway successes like *War Horse* or chestnuts like *Cats* trumping locally produced work." But just as a local production of *War Horse* doesn't direct itself, a touring exhibition doesn't simply transfer from one location to the next in a simple or predictable way. In the case of touring exhibitions, the primary task of the curator is seemingly already done, since the objects have been pre-selected for display (in this case by Reichmann). According to Laurel MacMillan, TIFF's Director of Exhibitions and

Kubrick and curation 11

SK:TE's co-curator, site-specific curators are afforded very little agency in selecting archival materials—the exhibition contents ship directly from location to location, and curators aren't able to request additional materials from the SKA; by the same token, they are not obligated to display every object they receive.[3] (For instance, a large neon reproduction of Kubrick's signature was prominently featured in other mountings of the exhibition but was conspicuously absent from TIFF's presentation.) The curatorial decisions, then, relate entirely to how they choose to organize and present the objects they are given, what they choose to add (e.g., a large replica of the monolith from *2001*), and how they design the exhibition space. Aside from a request directly from the Kubrick estate that the director's debut feature *Fear and Desire* be excluded from TIFF's retrospective screening program, TIFF was free to organize and contextualize the materials originally selected by Reichmann as they saw fit.[4]

For Jesse Wente, TIFF's Director of Film Programmes and co-curator of *SK:TE*, the primary goal was to tell a story: "When we're doing an exhibition, we know what the physical objects are that we can display, it sort of becomes 'What story do those things begin to tell?'[. . .] [Kubrick] himself as an artist denied explaining anything he did [. . .] that leaves it open to so much possible curation or curatorial approaches."[5] Having seen the Los Angeles staging of the exhibition at the LA County Museum of Art (LACMA), which organized its materials by theme rather than by film, Wente was compelled to present the material in a more regimented way that would force visitors to follow Kubrick's development as a filmmaker chronologically.[6] In other words, Wente sought to take visitors on a *narrative* journey: "Let's tell *his* story, through the films; so the best approach was not a thematic one but a chronological one." The HSBC Gallery space on the main floor of the Lightbox was thus divided in such a way that visitors would necessarily move from one film to the next in chronological order, beginning with *Fear and Desire* and ending with *Eyes Wide Shut*.[7]

The chronological approach is more in line with historical museums explicitly designed to serve a memorializing function (e.g., Holocaust museums) than traditional art exhibitions.[8] On the organization of materials in such spaces, Laura Houston Hanks (2012, 27) claims that "Choice is all but removed from the visitor, and other than by backtracking within the restricted space or taking one of the few shortcuts to the exit, the visitor is compelled to go in one direction, along with the crowd." Especially compared to the more explicitly interpretative approach taken at LACMA, this organizational strategy gives the impression of historical fact and thereby seems to offer a more "objective" portrait of the filmmaker and his career, drawing upon the institutional authority of the science or history museum rather than (or in addition to) the cultural capital of the art gallery. But as

Wente suggests above, they're also telling a story; the curator thus becomes a kind of "trustworthy and 'omniscient narrator'" (Hanks 2012, 31), using architecture to control pacing, sound and color to set different moods, and artifacts and expository object labels to provide narration. Though the power of the curator-as-auteur seems incompatible with Kubrick's own need for total control over his films and their presentation, Wente and MacMillan use that curatorial power to reassert and prioritize the artistic agency of Kubrick, the auteur-as-curator. This is similar but more precise than James Fenwick's (2017) observation that Kubrick exhibitions tend to "deify Kubrick and his films, motivated in large by the fandom of their curators." For instance, TIFF's mounting is ostentatiously aestheticized in its design, but specifically in ways that are meant to immerse the spectator within the audio-visual design of Kubrick's films. Additionally, Kubrick himself is represented as a curatorial agent throughout, portraying his artistic process as one with significant ties to collection and curation.

Uncovering Kubrick's "Rosebud"

As part of *SK:TE*'s online promotion, a TIFF.net blog post asked "Which #Kubrick Artifact Gets Instagrammed Most?" Jack Torrance's typewriter from *The Shining* came in at #1, with the Korova Milkbar set from *A Clockwork Orange* at #2 and the "REDRUM" door from *The Shining* at #3. That these three artifacts were social media favorites is understandable, given their visual iconicity, but these aren't the most *significant* items on display in terms of their positioning within the exhibition. The item that is given pride of place in *SK:TE* is actually something not seen in any Kubrick film, though it was present on every set and shooting location: his chess set. The unassuming wooden board and playing pieces, encased in glass, greets the visitor even before they enter the exhibition proper, accompanied by a quotation from the filmmaker:

> *You sit at the board and suddenly your heart leaps.*
> *Your hand trembles to pick up the piece and move it.*
> *But what chess teaches you is that you must sit there*
> *calmly and think whether it's really a good idea*
> *and whether there are other, better ideas.*

The quotation implicitly frames chess not as a pleasant but essentially trivial pastime that Kubrick happened to enjoy on his film sets, but rather as a significant, meaningful, and ultimately revelatory object vis-à-vis his approach to filmmaking, which is thereby characterized as a rational, contemplative, and competitive decision-making process. In *SK:TE*, the chess

Kubrick and curation 13

set becomes Kubrick's "Rosebud"—not a lost childhood object per se, but an object that is portrayed as the key to unlocking an otherwise inaccessible psyche. LoBrutto (1997, 19) elaborates on the relationship between chess and filmmaking, and provides the context for TIFF's quotation:

Chess was more than a game to Stanley—it represented order, logic, perseverance, and self-discipline [...] Stanley inherited the chess player's persona, quiet but determined, intense and strong-minded, while he exerted his will on the other player [...] As he became experienced and skilled at the chessboard, he began to use it as a way of learning important life lessons. "Chess is an analogy," he later said. "It is a series of steps that you take one at a time and it's balancing resources against the problem, which in chess is time and in movies is time and money." As his instincts as an artist began to grow, they were shaped by the desire to explore all his choices and coolly weigh each decision, a lesson the long hours of chess taught him. "I used to play chess twelve hours a day. You sit at the board and suddenly your heart leaps."

TIFF excludes enough of this context that the chessboard's relationship to Kubrick's filmmaking is evocative rather than didactic, but its positioning at the outset of the exhibition charges it with outsize meaning. The only other objects that precede the visitor's entry into the gallery space are two golden award statuettes—an Academy Award and a Golden Lion—that seem to testify to the success of this chess-like approach to filmmaking.

The exhibition proper consists of 12 discrete but connected spaces: one devoted to "Early Films" (*Fear and Desire, Killer's Kiss, The Killing*), and then a single room for each subsequent film, with the exception of *2001: A Space Odyssey*, which is spread across two rooms. Most obviously, the square footage devoted to each film creates a kind of hierarchy of importance, with *2001* reigning supreme as Kubrick's towering artistic achievement and early films like *Killer's Kiss* being treated as mere stepping stones to later, more significant works.[9] Sandwiched between comparatively large spaces devoted to *A Clockwork Orange* and *The Shining*, SK:TE's chronological ordering does no favors to *Barry Lyndon*, for instance, which is overshadowed by these more popular and iconic films and whose relatively small square footage implicitly positions it as "minor Kubrick." Each room features a different combination of archival materials: some favor props and costumes while other emphasize production documents, correspondence, set photography, or foretexts (e.g., storyboards, shooting scripts), the unique combination of which—combined with TIFF's expository labels for each room—creates a statement about Kubrick and his artistic process at a particular moment in his career. For instance, the *Spartacus* room begins with a large photograph of Kubrick towering over the Spanish countryside on a large camera crane; to its right is the room label, which emphasizes the large scope of the project, Kubrick's inexperience with studio filmmaking, and the young director's perfectionism. Elaborate and colorful storyboards by Saul Bass testify to the project's massive scale (especially relative to the comparatively colorless rooms devoted to the preceding films, all of which were filmed in black-and-white); and finally, a large photograph of a battlefield strewn with individually numbered extras (the largest number I can make out in the photo is 296, suggesting upwards of 300 extras in the scene) speaks to Kubrick's attention to detail and the extent of his mastery over his films' mise-en-scène. Combined with the visual dazzle created by the presence of two elaborate costumes from the film, *Spartacus* becomes framed in *SK:TE* as a momentous achievement and a key turning point in Kubrick's career—despite the director's stated ambivalence about the project.[10]

By contrast, the next two rooms—devoted to *Lolita* and *Dr. Strangelove*, respectively—emphasize public debates over the films' content, positioning Kubrick as a figure of controversy during the early 1960s; unsurprisingly, the positioning of the archival materials presented in these rooms encourages the conclusion that Kubrick was on the right side of history in these debates. For instance, the room label for *Lolita* concludes with the following: "Upon release **Lolita** received an 'X' rating in the UK, and while passed by the MPAA in America, the Catholic Church's Legion of Decency initially branded the film with a 'Condemned' rating, thus making it a sin for Catholics to see it. **Lolita** was an instant box-office hit." Letters to Kubrick by Christian decency groups—uniformly written in advance of the film's release—protest the very concept of a film based on Nabokov's novel, suggesting that such an endeavor would necessarily have a "deletorious [sic] effect upon our society." Kubrick's personal response to one of these letters expresses polite contempt for the collective pre-judging of his film, citing his previous artistic achievements as evidence that he has earned the benefit of the doubt. In the *Strangelove* room, a letter informing Kubrick that the film had been banned by censors in Portugal for its "political nature" sits beside a telegram from the head of marketing for Columbia Pictures in which he thanks the director for "making Columbias [sic] year so successful"; a personal letter to Kubrick from a disgruntled viewer describing the film's representation of the military as "despicable" is positioned adjacent to a telegram featuring raves about the film from the likes of Eli Wallach and Peter Fonda. In both cases, negative moralistic responses to Kubrick films are juxtaposed against more objective measures (box-office success) and what we are meant to perceive as more progressive (and therefore preferred) responses to their artistic content.

The aesthetic design of each individual room is also central to *SK:TE*'s effect on visitors. Generally speaking, the rooms are crafted in ways that are meant to immerse the visitor in the distinct audio-visual design of Kubrick's narrative worlds. For instance, the red walls of the *Spartacus* room evoke the film's marketing materials, which is particularly jarring following the greyscale of the two preceding rooms. Additionally, *Lolita*'s soft pink walls (adorned with a red painting of Lolita's heart-shaped glasses); *2001*'s antiseptic white; *A Clockwork Orange*'s orange walls encasing a reproduction of the Korova Milkbar set; *The Shining*'s orange, brown, and crimson hexagonally patterned carpet; and *Eyes Wide Shut*'s deep purple are especially effective at immersing visitors in distinctly Kubrickian spaces. Completing the effect is a soundscape in which the most well-known musical cues from Kubrick's films compete for attention—I recall hearing music from *A Clockwork Orange* floating in over the walls while I was in the "Early Films" room during one of my visits—a feature that becomes particularly noticeable in the second *2001* room, which is soundproofed to replicate the cold silence of space (and much of the film).

Finally, upon exiting the *Eyes Wide Shut* room, the visitor is presented with a small screening space in which a montage film—online, this would likely be passed around as a "supercut"—makes connections between shots, imagery, and camera movements from across Kubrick's filmography. The film, which was conceptualized and edited by Wente specifically for TIFF, is called "Perpetual Check," a callback to the chess set with which *SK:TE* began. So just as *Citizen Kane* begins with the mysterious evocation of Rosebud and ends with the revelation of its meaning, so too does *SK:TE* come back around to chess as a means of tying Kubrick's films together and perhaps even explaining his filmmaking mastery.

Perpetual check: Kubrick as collector/curator

As Siegelaub (2014, 36) puts it, "In an exhibition situation the context—other artists, specific works—begins to imply, from without, certain things about any artwork. The less standard the exhibition situation becomes, the more difficult to 'see' the individual work of art." It becomes difficult to see curated objects on their own, divorced from the context in which they have been so deliberately placed. Ostentatiously curated and obviously aestheticized exhibitions—and I would classify *SK:TE* among them—may thereby run the risk of being "seen as the exhibition-maker's own *Gesamtkunstwerk*" (a German concept that refers to an all-encompassing or universal artwork) with "the curator as an overriding figure or *auteur* who uses artwork to illustrate his or her own theory" (Obrist 2014, 32–33). In the case of *SK:TE*, the chess set functions as a kind of initial hypothesis that "Perpetual Check" ultimately confirms. *SK:TE* is best understood then not as an unmediated representation of Kubrick but rather as MacMillan and Wente's theory of Kubrick, their attempt to make sense of the intangible filmmaker: their *Gesamtkunstwerk*. What's clever about this argument and their overall approach to the exhibition, however, is that it uses their curatorial power in a self-effacing way. Just as the aestheticization of *SK:TE*'s various rooms seems to place visitors within specifically Kubrickian worlds rather than curatorial worlds, so too does the chess thesis function to position Kubrick as a kind of *ur*curator, the initial and chief interlocutor behind the exhibition. His interest in and mastery of chess conceptualizes the filmmaker as a master thinker and long-term strategist, always thinking many moves ahead in order to manipulate his opponent into fulfilling his own design. By this logic, *SK:TE* becomes the endgame—or perhaps just another move in a still ongoing game—of a process Kubrick himself set in motion with the mov(i)es he made during his life. While undeniably hyperbolic, such an outsize understanding of Kubrick's genius is perfectly in keeping with contemporary popular discourse about the filmmaker; for instance, the various interpretations of *The Shining* offered in the documentary *Room 237* (2012) all rest upon the paradoxical assumption that even Kubrick's *mistakes* (e.g., continuity errors) are deliberate and ripe with hidden meaning.

I have established the means through which this theory of Kubrick bookends *SK:TE*, but how does this argument manifest within the exhibition itself? In my view, it is done by portraying Kubrick's filmmaking practice as an art with strong ties to collection and curation. As described by Walter Benjamin (1999, 9), collectors divest the objects they collect of their use value, which they replace with "connoisseur value." Benjamin refers to this as the "transfiguration" of objects, the redemption of things as such apart from their use value. The expansiveness of Kubrick's collection as represented by the SKA, the touring exhibition, and *SK:TE* all suggest that he was an obsessive collector (if not an outright hoarder). This characteristic is not a new revelation: writing about Kubrick's Porsche, biographer John Baxter (1997, 299) claims that "nobody ever saw [the car] out of the yard. Like Kubrick's radios, stereos, TVs, cameras and projectors, it was a trophy, a collectible: the best of its kind, state of the art, just as valuable to him and an equal source of pleasure if it stayed in the garage." *SK:TE*, however, suggests that this is not an accurate characterization of Kubrick's collecting. As Hans Ulrich Obrist (2014, 39) writes,

> To make a collection is to find, acquire, organize and store items, whether in a room, a house, a library, a museum or a warehouse. It is also, inevitably, a way of thinking about the world—the connections and principles

that produce a collection contain assumptions, juxtapositions, findings, experimental possibilities and associations. Collection-making, you could say, is a method of producing knowledge.

By this logic—that of the *curator* rather than the Benjaminian collector—Kubrick didn't collect objects and knowledge with the intent of merely creating personal "cabinets of curiosity" for his own enjoyment, but rather in order to turn them into films: his own *Gesamtkunstwerk*.
Kubrick's collection of objects accumulated primarily during the preproduction phase of filmmaking. For each film, and increasingly over the course of his career, Kubrick would research thoroughly in order to make himself a student of his subject. He then put this collected knowledge to use in the writing (or commissioning) of screenplays, in the scouting of locations, in the directing of actors. *SK:TE* explicitly describes Kubrick's process in these terms: according to TIFF's section panel introducing the *Napoleon* area, Kubrick hired "20 grad students to compile research and [create] a voluminous card catalogue that detailed every single day of Napoleon's life." One object that Wente singles out as particularly significant is the filing card cabinet that houses the fruits of this research, recorded on countless cards that are carefully arranged across 12 drawers. For Wente, this cabinet functions as "physical evidence" that certain myths about Kubrick's obsessive perfectionism were objectively true. The object label for the cabinet asserts that "These research materials and their complex organizational strategy testify not only to the magnitude of the project but also to the meticulous preparation that Kubrick undertook." (Or more casually, in Wente's words: "That cabinet is the work of a chess master.") There's a story being told here—not merely by the object itself but the object in conjunction with Kubrick's mythology and the explicit interpretation provided by the object label: before making an artistic decision, Kubrick required every possible option to choose from—one can imagine him test-driving every last car on the lot before settling on the Porsche—in order to make the best possible choice. Thus the creation of a collection, a vast storehouse of artistic possibilities, is represented as an integral part of his filmmaking process. Ultimately these objects and this knowledge exist only to be pared down and organized: the films he made (and came close to making) are curated from these collections. Kubrick's curator-like filmmaking process comes across throughout the exhibition: in the hand-written annotations of the novels he selected for adaptation, his correspondence with collaborators and potential collaborators, in letters written to theaters ensuring that they're screening his films according to his exact specifications, and in the unused poster treatments for films like *A Clockwork Orange* and *The Shining* (the latter of which feature hand-written commentary from Kubrick to Saul Bass). In

short, the Kubrick whose story is told in *SK:TE* is an artist whose process and responsibilities are not so different from those of a curator. He collects; he solicits work from others; he interprets, synthesizes, and creates; he markets that creation; and finally, he ensures that it is exhibited properly.

Exit through the gift shop

Robert J.E. Simpson (2008) suggests that the Kubrick's legacy will be torn between the late director himself, his estate, critics and historians, and the film buffs that will collect the commodities and experiences that are curated for them, including the traveling exhibition. This struggle for control over Kubrick's afterlife may be best embodied in the gift shop that accompanied *SK:TE*. It's commonly believed that "Museum gift shops, postcards, and the common reproduction of art in newspapers and magazines served to rapidly liquidate the sanctity of art" in a transparent and potentially crass way (Wasson 2005, 186). For TIFF's gift shop, rights restrictions (presumably from Warner Bros.) prevented the sale of merchandise with imagery taken from the films themselves, so many of the original items relate back instead to the literary source materials, including *A Clockwork Orange* mugs and tote bags and a *Lolita* baby-tee. Despite these restrictions, TIFF sold knit beanie caps adorned with the memorable carpet pattern of *The Shining*'s Overlook Hotel, as well as a reasonable facsimile of Danny's "Apollo 11" knit sweater from the same film. Walk upstairs to TIFF's Luma bar and you could even order a "Kubrick Cocktail."[11]

Rather than decry these attempts at further monetizing Kubrick, I would connect these commodities—all of which were either commissioned or curated by TIFF specifically for their Kubrick exhibition—to broader trends in how film auteurs circulate throughout the world, both in physical spaces and online, as concepts or aesthetics rather than individuals. Indeed, the term "Kubrickian" was recently added to the Oxford English Dictionary, a move that represents Kubrick's ultimate transcendence from human being to pure concept.[12] The reality of postmodern media culture is that more people will encounter *2001: A Space Odyssey* through homages on *The Simpsons* than projected in 70mm. Appropriations such as these disseminate a director's work in a way that traditional auteur studies typically exclude from their analyses, but we can no longer ignore their significance. In seeking the "authorial voice" of a director, either in their films or through the resources of an archive, we risk overlooking secondary texts that what may very well represent the primary ways in which filmmakers reverberate through contemporary media culture. When you wear your *Shining* beanie on a cold winter's day, you too contribute to the real-time dissemination and evolution of Kubrick's cultural reverberation

Kubrick and curation 19

in a similar way. In a real sense, you become a paratext to *The Shining*, performing work that is different in degree but not in kind from TIFF's exhibition.

Notes

1 Georgia Clemson (Archives and Special Collections Assistant), email message to author, November 3, 2016. These numbers roughly correlate with those presented by Richard Daniels in his essay "The Stanley Kubrick Archive: A Filmmaker's Legacy": "from August 2015 to end of July 2016, there were nearly two thousand visitors; of them 90 percent viewed the Kubrick Archive in some way. Just over 50 percent of them were internal, i.e. students or staff members of University of the Arts London" (Daniels 2017).
2 TIFF did program a retrospective screening series, "Stanley Kubrick: A Filmmaking Odyssey," that coincided with *SK:TE*'s run at the Lightbox and included the premiere screening of a newly struck 70mm print of *2001: A Space Odyssey*.
3 Laurel MacMillan in conversation with the author, March 3, 2016.
4 Why the Kubrick estate requested that *Fear and Desire* be excluded from the retrospective is unclear, but is consistent with Kubrick's attempts to bury the film during his lifetime.
5 Jesse Wente in conversation with the author, February 25, 2016. All subsequent quotations from Wente come from this unpublished interview.
6 As James Fenwick (2017) notes, all pre-LA mountings of the exhibition were, like TIFF's, organized chronologically.
7 An additional gallery on the fourth floor of the Lightbox was open to the public without the purchase of a ticket. On display were a less regimented assortment of material that didn't neatly fit into this chronological schema, including a gallery of one-sheets from around the world, a collection of Kubrick's camera equipment and lenses, his photographic output for *Look* Magazine, and archival material relating to unfinished film projects like *A.I.: Artificial Intelligence, Aryan Papers,* and *Napoleon*.
8 Thanks to Kass Banning for pointing this out to me based on an earlier version of this chapter.
9 The relegation of *Killer's Kiss* extends to its treatment on home video as well, where its most recent and definitive release positions it as a bonus feature on The Criterion Collection's *The Killing* disc. See Jeffries 2017.
10 See, for instance, Kubrick's comments in Michel Ciment's *Kubrick: The Definitive Edition*: "In *Spartacus* I tried with only limited success to make the film as [historically] real as possible but I was up against a pretty dumb script which was rarely faithful to what is known about Spartacus [. . .] If I ever needed any convincing of the limits of persuasion a director can have on a film where someone else is the producer and he is merely the highest-paid member of the crew, then *Spartacus* provided proof to last a lifetime" (quoted in Cooper 2007, 57).
11 I myself sampled the "A Clockwork Blood Orange" cocktail, containing Beefeater gin, Aperol, and Aranciata Rossa. See https://twitter.com/TIFF_NET/status/537350665270734848 for the complete menu.
12 The Dictionary defines "Kubrickian" as "meticulous perfectionism, mastery of the technical aspects of filmmaking, and atmospheric visual style in films across a range of genres." See Reilly 2018.

Works cited

Balzer, David. 2014. *Curationism: How Curating Took over the Art World and Everything Else*. Toronto: Coach House Books.
Baxter, John. 1997. *Stanley Kubrick: A Biography*. New York: Carroll & Graf Publishers.
Benjamin, Walter. 1999. *The Arcades Project*. Translated by Howard Eiland and Kevin McLaughlin. Cambridge, MA: The Belknap Press of Harvard University Press.
Broderick, Mick. 2017. "Post-Kubrick: On the Filmmaker's Influence and Legacy." *Screening the Past*, no. 42. www.screeningthepast.com/2017/09/post-kubrick-on-the-filmmakers-influence-and-legacy/.
Buren, Daniel. 2014. "Exhibiting Exhibitions." In *Exhibition*, edited by Lucy Steeds, 43–44. Cambridge, MA: The MIT Press.
Cooper, Duncan L. 2007. "Dalton Trumbo vs. Stanley Kubrick: The Historical Meaning of Spartacus." In *Spartacus: Film and History*, edited by Martin M. Winkler, 56–64. Malden, MA: Blackwell Publishing.
Daniels, Richard. 2017. "The Stanley Kubrick Archive: A Filmmaker's Legacy." *Screening the Past*, no. 42. www.screeningthepast.com/2017/09/the-stanley-kubrick-archive-a-filmmakers-legacy/.
Fenwick, James. 2017. "Curating Kubrick: Constructing New Perspective Narratives in Stanley Kubrick Exhibitions." *Screening the Past*, no. 42. www.screeningthepast.com/2017/09/curating-kubrick-constructing-new-perspective-narratives-in-stanley-kubrick-exhibitions/.
Gray, Jonathan. 2010. *Show Sold Separately: Promos, Spoilers, and Other Media Paratexts*. New York: New York University Press.
Hancock, Nuala. 2010. "Virginia Woolf's Glasses: Material Encounters in the Literary/Artistic House Museum." In *Museum Materialities: Objects, Engagements, Interpretations*, edited by Sandra H. Dudley, 114–27. New York: Routledge.
Hanks, Laura Houston. 2012. "Writing Spatial Stories: Textual Narratives in the Museum." In *Museum Making: Narratives, Architecture, Exhibitions*, edited by Suzanne MacLeod, Laura Houston Hanks, and Jonathan Hale, 21–33. New York: Routledge.
Jeffries, Dru. 2017. "Owning Kubrick: The Criterion Collection and the Ghost in the Auteur Machine." *Cinergie* 12. https://doi.org/10.6092/issn.2280-9481/7339.
Kim, Jihoon. 2017. "Stanley Kubrick in the Museum: Post-Cinematic Conditions, Limitations, and Possibilities." *Curator: The Museum Journal* 60, no. 4: 467–87.
Ljujić, Tatjana, Peter Krämer, and Richard Daniels. 2015. "Introduction." In *Stanley Kubrick: New Perspectives*, edited by Tatjana Ljujić, Peter Krämer, and Richard Daniels, 13–19. London: Black Dog Publishing.
LoBrutto, Vincent. 1997. *Stanley Kubrick: A Biography*. New York: Donald I. Fine Books.
Ng, David. 2013. "Stanley Kubrick at LACMA Was Popular, but Not Like Tim Burton." *Los Angeles Times*, July 10. http://articles.latimes.com/2013/jul/10/entertainment/la-et-cm-stanley-kubrick-lacma-attendance-20130709.
Obrist, Hans Ulrich. 2014. *Ways of Curating*. London: Penguin Group.

O'Neill, Paul. 2012. *The Culture of Curating and the Curating of Culture(s)*. Cambridge, MA: The MIT Press.
Polan, Dana. 2001. "Auteur Desire." *Screening the Past*, no. 12. https://web.archive.org/web/20010419103933/www.latrobe.edu.au/www/screeningthepast/firstrelease/fr0301/dpfr12a.htm.
Reichmann, Hans-Peter. 2014. "Real Is Good, Interesting Is Better." In *Stanley Kubrick*. 3rd ed., edited by Deutsches Filmmuseum, 9–12. Frankfurt: Deutsches Filmmuseum.
Reilly, Nick. 2018. " 'Lynchian', 'Tarantinoesque' and 'Kubrickian' Lead New Film Words Added to Oxford English Dictionary." *NME*, October 5. www.nme.com/news/film/lynchian-tarantinoesque-and-kubrickian-lead-new-film-words-added-to-oxford-english-dictionary-definition-2387041.
Siegelaub, Seth. 2014. "On Exhibitions and the World at Large: In Conversation with Charles Harrison." In *Exhibition*, edited by Lucy Steeds, 36–40. Cambridge, MA: The MIT Press.
Simpson, Robert J. E. 2008. "Whose Stanley Kubrick? The Myth, Legacy, and Ownership of the Kubrick Image." In *Stanley Kubrick: Essays on His Films and Legacy*, edited by Gary D. Rhodes, 232–44. Jefferson, NC: McFarland & Company, Inc. Publishers.
Steeds, Lucy. 2014. "Introduction // Contemporary Exhibitions: Art at Large in the World." In *Exhibition*, edited by Lucy Steeds, 12–23. Cambridge, MA: The MIT Press.
Wasson, Haidee. 2005. *Museum Movies: The Museum of Modern Art and the Birth of Art Cinema*. Berkeley, CA: University of California Press.
Whitehead, Christopher. 2012. *Interpreting Art in Museums and Galleries*. New York: Routledge.

3 The rise of Doctor Strangelove

Stanley Kubrick, Peter George, Herman Kahn, and a new world morality

Graham Allen

By first moving back to pre-production material, and then pushing forwards to subsequent texts, this essay is an attempt to assess the legacy of Kubrick's classic nuclear film, *Dr. Strangelove or: How I Learned to Stop Worrying and Love the Bomb* (1964). The paper contributes to the recent reassessment of the role of author Peter George in the Strangelove project. Over the years there has been confusion over the scripting of this film (Broderick 2017, 32). Taking George's role more seriously than it has been in many past studies, I want to explore the influence of the work of the nuclear strategist Herman Kahn on both George and Kubrick. By looking at such a mutual influence we can come to a deeper understanding of the political and philosophical import of the film.[1]

This, then, sheds a number of new lights on our critical understanding of the influence the Strangelove project had on Kubrick's and George's subsequent work, especially with regards to their strikingly different and yet in many respects parallel returns to the film's abiding concern with human survival in *2001: A Space Odyssey* (1968) and *Commander-1* (1965). The latter text, George's deeply dystopian, post-apocalypse novel, is an extraordinarily important piece of evidence in the attempt to gauge his response to the material he worked on with Kubrick. *Commander-1* is an adaptation and expansion of the *Dr. Strangelove* project, and in extending Kubrick's thinking on nuclear warfare it provides *Dr. Strangelove* with a sequel that has ongoing relevance. *Commander-1*, in other words, is a novel which illuminates our approach to the film *Dr. Strangelove* and clarifies its ongoing legacy for our nuclear world. In order to work as a 'nightmare comedy,' the film was edited free of any explicit political or ideological statements. However, mining the archival record allows us a better insight into the socio-political legacy the larger Strangelove project still exerts, including its timely warning of how the apparent need for a new, post-nuclear, world morality can, in times of crisis, eventuate in the return of fascism. The legacy of Strangelove involves the reality of where we are and a warning of where we might be going.[2] To understand that present and potential future, however, we first must return to some of the origins of Strangelove.

The influence of Herman Kahn: versions of Dr. Strangelove

It is well known that Stanley Kubrick was influenced by Herman Kahn's *On Thermonuclear War*, as he worked on *Strangelove* (Ghamari-Tabrizi 2005, 275–77). We should remember, however, that Peter George's novel, *Red Alert*, actually appears for discussion within Kahn's famous treatise. Kahn wrote to George with enthusiasm about how *Red Alert* deals with the issue of nuclear war by accident and through the actions of unauthorized individuals (Ghamari-Tabrizi 2005, 276; Broderick 2017, 99). Nowadays it is common to see Herman Kahn as one of the direct models for the character of Dr. Strangelove. As Peter Krämer writes: "If there was a real-life model for the charismatic nuclear strategist with a best-selling book about nuclear war that Peter George and Kubrick were developing at the time, it was Herman Kahn" (Krämer 2014, 102). Mick Broderick takes a more inclusive approach, reminding us of the many strategic, scientific, political, and fictional influences standing behind the character's "evolution" (Broderick 2017, 46–96). However, of all these sources it is only Kahn who actively engaged in the development of the scripting of the film and only Kahn who felt sufficiently involved as to (unsuccessfully) make a claim for a share in writer's royalties (Ghamari-Tabrizi 2005, 41–42; Broderick 2017, 57–58).

On Thermonuclear War caused a great deal of controversy when it was first published in 1960. The book argues that it is a potentially catastrophic mistake to equate the idea of thermonuclear war with the complete annihilation of human civilization. Such thinking allows politicians and military top brass to simply rely on the bomb's apocalyptic threat, instead of developing complex strategy and investing in military operations and civilian defense programs (Kahn 2007, 8). In opposition to such a "comfortable" apocalypticism, Kahn urges us to "think about the unthinkable" (Kahn 2007, 116; Cordle 2008, 45–46). In this spirit, Kahn coolly discusses such previously taboo subjects as a U.S. first strike policy, the difference between targeting civilian and military targets, sacrificing parts of the country to insure the survival of others, the idea of city-swaps as limiting nuclear targets, and other unpalatable topics (Aligica and Weinstein 2009, 268). The possibilities for figuring Kahn as a monster are not difficult to imagine and were accepted and discussed by Kahn himself (Kahn 2007, 20–21).[3] In response to the severity of the attacks on *Thermonuclear War*, Kahn reiterated his points in his 1962 follow-up work, *Thinking About the Unthinkable* (Kaplan 1983, 228; Kahn 1962).

The most compelling evidence for Kahn's influence on the development of the film script comes from papers held in the Kubrick Archive. Richard Daniels has outlined the labyrinthine path, through serious and comic treatments (including "27 draft scripts and loose sheets of script modifications"), the co-writers took in adapting George's novel to film. Within these various scripts, treatments, and notes we see a recurrent focus on Kahn. There are direct references to him, as when, in a script titled "Red Alert" and dated March 1, 1962, the pilot says to a skeptical bombardier: "Don't start trying to become another Herman Kahn" (SKA/11/1/15). There are numerous direct allusions to the text of *On Thermonuclear War*, but there are also more indirect allusions to what we might call the Kahnian discourse of assertion through the stockpiling of questions.[4] In a more sustained way, we might look at the scripts, treatments, and notes associated with the March to June 1962 narrative entitled "The Rise of Doctor Strangelove." This is a comic narrative in which Strangelove rises to become profoundly powerful as the top U.S. government nuclear strategist. Much is made here of the concept, strongly associated with Kahn, of the potential cost of nuclear war in megadeaths. The Kahn connection is deepened through the fact that Strangelove's notoriety is based on his having authored an influential book, in some texts entitled "The Facts About Nuclear War" and then, more tellingly still, in other texts entitled "Man Into Numbers" (SK/11.1.15, SK/11/1/16 and SK/11/1/16).

One isolated, hand-written question in SK/11/1/16 runs: "Should Strangelove be President?" In another fascinating loose typed sheet, entitled "Election Eve—1—, " Strangelove (his face depicted on a "Giant Poster" underneath which is written the Orwellian sentence "Knowledge is Power") is actually elected President, after the Republican party, in order to stop a "Democratic landslide," has selected him as a surprise candidate. In this account, Walter Cronkite comments: "Strangelove reduced the campaign issues to a single theme: Survival In The Nuclear Age, and he obviously impressed the electorate that he was the man to insure survival" (SKA/11/1/17). A note at the bottom of the page emphasizes the role Strangelove's book "Man Into Numbers" has in his rise to power: "This highly, controversial book, attacked and praised with equal vigor, has been described as a cool objective look into hell. Etc. (whatever we want to make of the book)." So here Kahn à la Strangelove becomes U.S. President by exploiting the fear raised about nuclear war in his own book.

When we examine Kahn's influence on Kubrick's finished film, we see that the famous theorist of the Doomsday Machine has an influence that is not limited to the character of Strangelove (Kahn 2007, 145–54). Indeed, Kahn's text seems to have spread out to influence or infect many of the film's characters. General Buck Turgidson and the President have as many quotations from *On Thermonuclear War* woven into their speeches as Strangelove. Turgidson's "admittedly regrettable but nevertheless distinguishable post-war environments" alludes to a table early on in the first lecture of Kahn's book: "Tragic But Distinguishable Postwar States" (Kahn 2007, 34). His references to "an all-out slugging match" and to a Soviet "sneak attack" have their counterparts in *On Thermonuclear War* (Kahn 2007, 186, 239, 258, 271). Perhaps more importantly his speech about "acceptable losses" as calculated in megadeaths is a significant feature of *On Thermonuclear War*, as we have seen, and would no doubt have been recognized as such by a portion of Kubrick's original audience (Kahn 2007, 19–21).[5]

Turgidson often utters a Kahnian rhetoric. But then so does President Muffley. His question whether "the survivors will envy the dead" is taken directly from a long section of Kahn's first lecture (Kahn 2007, 40–95). Kahn's discussions of the problems of arms control between the superpowers is reflected in a number of the speeches given to the President but ultimately cut from the film edit (Broderick, 176–7). President Muffley's comic attempts to calm his drunken Soviet counterpart on the other end of the phone seem inspired by Kahn's run through of typical phrases and approaches made by those non-military leaders shocked at the prospect of nuclear carnage. The first paraphrased reaction reads: "1. *The problem is hypothetical*. You cannot *prove* it exists. *There is no need to get hysterical*" (Kahn 2007, 347 emphasis added). Is there a criticism of President Muffley being made through this covert allusion, or are Kubrick and George simply ransacking Kahn's text as an available source for material? It is difficult to say at times.

At other times things seem a little clearer, as in the case of President Muffley's reference to Hitler: "I am not going to go down in history as the greatest mass murderer since Adolf Hitler." This statement is clearly taken from Kahn's text where he writes: "Almost nobody wants to go down in history as the first man to kill 100,000,000 people" (Kahn 2007, 171). The context of Kahn's remark is that it is extremely dangerous for leaders, military or civilian, to continue to think of warfare in terms of World War II. The fact is the nuclear bomb has completely altered the nature of warfare: its planning, its conduct, and its after effects. Kahn reflects on how civilians were turned into targets during World War II but how such an approach is radically questioned in the age of thermonuclear war.[6]

Of course, none of the above is to suggest that the character of Strangelove himself is not saturated in the rhetoric of *On Thermonuclear War*. Readers coming to Kahn's text after having seen the film (which, after the book's initial success and notoriety, has been the majority) cannot help but hear the half-crazed tones of Peter Sellers in much of what Kahn writes. In discussing one of his book's most persistent themes, what we might call *survivability*, Kahn sounds like Strangelove: "It would not surprise me," he writes, "if the overwhelming majority of survivors devoted themselves with a somewhat fanatical intensity to the task of rebuilding what was destroyed" (Kahn 2007, 90). Similarly, when Kahn imagines "normal and happy lives for the majority of survivors and their descendants" we hear Strangelove (Kahn 2007, 21). When Kahn imagines due preparations allowing the U.S. or the Soviets to "cope with all the effects of thermonuclear war, in the sense of saving most people and returning to something close to the prewar standard of living in a relatively short time" we hear Strangelove (Kahn 2007, 71). When he discusses the utility of available mineshaft space to store a portion of the U.S. population during the worst period of fallout, we hear Strangelove.[7] When Kahn discusses the idea of a Doomsday device, we hear Strangelove (mixed with a portion of de Sadesky) (Kahn 2007, 145, 147).

This influence and two-way contamination extends beyond the film to Peter George's 1963 novel *Dr. Strangelove* (George 2015). During the increasingly frantic negotiations with the Soviet Premier, General Turgidson passes a book under the President's nose. It is entitled *World Targets in Megadeaths* and is clearly a less than subtle allusion to *On Thermonuclear War* (George 2015, 152–53).[8] More tellingly still, as the crew of the Leper Colony (originally the Alabama Angel) receive the command to go to Wing Attack Plan R, the narrator states: "There were a few moments of absolute silence while they *thought about the unthinkable*" (George 2015, 25, emphasis added).[9] The allusion widens the scope of Kahn's audience (that audience encouraged to *think about the unthinkable*) to a group of military operatives normally expected to follow orders rather than to think independently.

Our reading is enhanced further if we proceed to two far more significant elements of George's text. The first concerns George's restoration of and in parts expansion of President Muffley's summative speeches, which formed a decisive late cut in Kubrick's editing of the film (Broderick 2017, 176–77). The President's angry reaction to de Sadesky's refusal to pray in thanks for their apparent deliverance from Armageddon, provokes him into criticisms of the Soviet's responses to disarmament talks which have some of their sources in Kahn's discussions of that subject (Kahn 2007, 224, 234, 245–46). Talking heatedly about how the invention of nuclear weapons makes any level of mutual trust between the super powers an insufficient safeguard, the President concludes: "Even disarmament is not enough. We can never entirely get rid of the Bomb because the knowledge of how to make it will always now be with us. Unless we learn to create a new system of law and morality between nations then we will exterminate ourselves, just as we almost did today" (George 2015, 143).

The idea of establishing a "new system of law and morality" is a key element in George's response to Kahn's work here.[10] It introduces a theme that is thinly referenced but never properly developed in *On Thermonuclear War*. At the commencement of his book, for example, Kahn writes: "I believe that even a poor world government might be preferable to an uncontrolled arms race, I also believe that the practical difficulties are so large that it is a digression to dwell on such possibilities as a possible solution for the problem of the sixties" (Kahn 2007, 7). The statement is rather perplexing, in that a world government is raised as necessary but is then, because of its difficulties (how do we get from here [the cold war] to there [world government], relegated to a "digression."[11]

But what kind of "world government" is being offered up here as at once a solution and yet a digression in the face of nuclear realities? In thinking the issue through again, in the final, futurological sections of his book, Kahn ends up reflecting: "I do not know if it is possible to explain to a democratic public the rationality and necessity for being willing to fight limited wars. If it is not possible, I predict a very dim future for democracy in our troubled era" (Kahn 2007, 529). The prospect opens up at the end of Kahn's book, therefore, of "a new system of law and morality" which seems less new than one might wish. It is this sense haunting Kahn's text of a darkening future, and the return, in new forms, of dictatorship and fascism, that George appears to pick up on in his expansion of the character of Strangelove.

On first reading George's novel version, it might appear that he is struggling to incorporate the figure of Dr. Strangelove in a narratively vital way. But it is worth looking again at his brief yet accumulating interpolations of Strangelove into the scene, since what becomes clear is the way in which they establish around him the theme of the new impending epoch. They make it clear that Strangelove is "not displeased" that the situation seems irresolvable (George 2015, 52, 91, 110). These brief interpolations also make clear the association being drawn between Strangelove and Kahn. As the narrator states: "He was of course familiar with the jargon of the nuclear strategists. Indeed, he himself had created a great deal of it" (George 2015, 66). In fact, expanding upon the largely implicit clues from the film, George's Strangelove is a strategist with a plan, a plan to help establish a new world order: "He didn't think these fools would ever succeed in destroying the last plane. He looked away and concentrated more than ever on his scheme to save at least a nucleus of specimens of the human race" (George 2015, 155).[12] The reference to "specimens" is telling. In order to hammer home the point, George has Strangelove repeat the term "human specimens" so many times in his exchange with the President that the latter begins to demonstrate visible anger and frustration with his odd interlocutor (George 2015, 175). But this is the dawn of the epoch for which Strangelove has been waiting so expectantly and, as George enters into his version of the discussion about mineshaft living, the film's associations of Nazism with Strangelove are expanded upon, culminating in their exchange about survivors:

> The President said thoughtfully: "But only several hundred saved. There would be panic, rioting, absolute chaos."
> Strangelove said, "I am sure the armed forces could deal with any disobedience. Men cannot fight against tanks and machine guns, Mister President. This we have proved."
>
> (George 2015, 178)

The collective pronoun in that last statement is chilling. Peter Seller's "My Fuhrer! I can walk!" is explicitly reworked in George's version as the arrival of a fascist epoch of the protected few and the surviving human "remnant." More importantly still, this rise of Strangelove's fascist epoch is also demonstrated to be one possible (maybe likely) outcome of a Kahnian doctrine of nuclear survivability, and thus feasible nuclear conflict. George's novel engages implicitly and explicitly with Kahn, not to accuse him of outright fascism, but to warn that a military-based dictatorship, rather than a benign, peace-loving "world government," is a likely outcome of his arguments about winnable nuclear conflicts and the survivability of such conflicts. The question both film and novel ask of their versions of Strangelove, in other words, is not whether nuclear war is survivable, but what form of future society is such a war likely to create?

This reading of George's Strangelove novel is usefully supplemented by reference to his treatment of the backstory for the Strangelove character that he wrote in late Spring 1962 as part of the "Rise of Doctor Strangelove" version (Krämer 2014, 70).[13]

Here, in a text which links Strangelove even more directly with Kahn, Strangelove becomes the tool of a military industrial complex keen to prop up "moron" puppet Presidents and to find ever more compelling arguments that nuclear weapons create peace so long as they are manufactured, along with a healthy Kahn-inspired civil defense program, at rates that keep the economy booming. George's political understanding of how the United States had become economically dependent upon the nuclear industry is astute, worthy indeed of comparison with Kahn's own brand of futurology. It ends by returning to what I am arguing both Kubrick and George saw as the most dangerous aspect of Kahnian rhetoric, that is the idea that nuclear war is not only winnable but that such a kind of war is compatible with humane values. The new "moron" President here is propped up with Strangelove's new "theory of war," which is so convincing, and so clean compared to previous non-nuclear wars, that even the enemy agrees with it (George 2015, 213–14).

Surviving Strangelove: *Commander-1*

At the end of his preface to *On Thermonuclear War*, Kahn writes: "I have a firm belief that unless we have more serious and sober thought on various facets of the strategic problem that seems to be typical of most discussion today . . . we are not going to reach the year 2000—and maybe not even the year 1965—without a cataclysm of some sort, and that this cataclysm will prove a lot more cataclysmic than it needs to be" (Kahn 2007, xviii). Whether Kubrick and Clarke's choice of the year 2001 for their science fiction project is in any way a response to Kahn's prediction is difficult to say. What is clear is that Kubrick's most famous film presents a return to the perspective of the alien frame-narrative that the writers of *Dr. Strangelove* had contemplated, and which George reinstates in his Strangelove novel (see script August 31, 1962 in SK/11/1/18 and George 2015, 5–8, 182). It is also not difficult to see, as Peter Krämer reminds us, that the entire *2001* project is haunted by the shadow of nuclear cataclysm (Krämer 2010, 13–17). In Clarke's novel, the star child that Bowman has transformed into detonates the "slumbering cargo of death" that is the world's (or half the world's) nuclear arsenal, preferring "a cleaner sky" (Clarke 1968, 252). The nuclear problem is thus solved through one human's evolution into a higher consciousness. Less explicit, the film allows at least for the possibility that Kahn's world government, despite obvious suspicions between American and Russian space travelers, is at least in the process of being established. However, as is often remarked, this "clean" technological future appears to have been accomplished at the expense of human spirit, imagination, and energy (Kroker 2011, 147). Thus Kubrick's film challenges us to ask the question: what are we prepared to lose about ourselves as humans for the sake of a safe technologically led future? The question is interestingly Kahnian and yet (in its emphasis on ineffable human qualities) rather unlike anything Kahn allows himself to ask, at least in *On Thermonuclear War*. There is no space here to explore Kahn's influence on Kubrick's *2001*. What can be said is that Kubrick's co-writer, Peter George, went on to explore just the question we are highlighting in his neglected, post-apocalyptic, nuclear novel, *Commander-1*.

Commander-1 is dedicated to Kubrick and is in many ways a continuation of the Strangelove story, particularly the narrative arc explored in the "Rise of Doctor Strangelove" material. The novel in fact, presents a realization of the implicit political vision of Kubrick's film and in so doing connects the "nightmare" vision of that film to our current circumstances. It is also, however, in the first of its three distinct parts, a conscious return to *Red Alert*. A Chinese plot (gradually revealed to readers) has precipitated a global cataclysm.[14] As the situation develops and shadowy Presidential Aides emerge to instruct the increasingly overwhelmed Generals, we witness an inexorable shift from elected to unelected power. This is then cut short by a switch in the second section of the novel to the journal of Commander James William Geraghty, of the U.S. Navy. This move promises many things, including the prospect that the swift cutting technique of the first part of the novel, with its consequent lack of stable focus, has been replaced by something more focused. The reader begins with the sense that Geraghty must be this novel's primary subject. We are entering, in other words, the comforting realm of the survivor's story. Geraghty's mission is to take six civilians (he calls them "guinea pigs"), three doctors, plus his crew, to a remote island and thereby test how the six subjects fare in isolation. The test, interestingly, is part of a plan to send humans to the planets, but as we lurch into December 25, 1965 and beyond, it is a test that is completely undermined by the nuclear conflict that has broken out. Unaccountably, however, Geraghty will not listen to the doctors' plea that they return to the U.S. to help the survivors, and the experience of reading his account of their voyage to the island becomes one of increasing doubt about the state of his mind and his ethical choices. Is Geraghty a good commander or a psychopath? The evidence builds of his unwavering patriotism (at times he sounds like *Red Alert/Dr. Strangelove's* General Quinten/Ripper), his almost complete aversion to physical relations between his crew (at times he sounds like Colonel 'Bat' Guano), and ultimately his no less than concealed racism and homophobia. By the time we reach the island it has become evident to the reader that Geraghty is a white supremacist, military dictator in the making. Our initial empathy with him, elicited largely through narrative conventions and expectations, has once again demonstrated how fascism in its domestic forms can wear the most plausible and unassuming masks. This process of unveiling Geraghty's true nature, so deftly achieved by George, is coincident with Geraghty's rise (not yet fully unveiled at this stage) to position of Commander-1, post-apocalyptic world leader. In other words, it parallels the displacement of democratically elected government with an unelected military regime. What appears to be a possibility at the end of *Dr. Strangelove*, and is even more directly inferred in the "Rise of Doctor Strangelove" texts, plays out before our eyes, as we struggle to make sense of events and of key characters. There is still some distance for the first-time reader to travel before all this is fully revealed, however.

Here we enter the novel's third distinct section, with the focus switching to the six civilian survivors left to fend for themselves on the island. They deduce that the island is in the best position to avoid the fall out created by the war, although it is unclear without radiation meters whether the air is clean or contaminated.[15] The whole scenario brings us back to Kahn's prolonged speculations about nuclear survival, including his question already reiterated by Peter Sellers' President Muffley: "Will the Survivors Envy the Dead?" In particular, as the three men and three women form into couples, the question in the absence of contraception lands on Kahn's notorious discussions of the effects of radiation on children. Kahn's discussions of the probable rates of infant deformity due to different radiation levels, leads in *On Thermonuclear War* to his account of a woman in the audience at one of his lectures who had objected: "I don't want to live in a world in which 1 percent of the children are born defective." Kahn's reply, that she already lives in a world where 4% of children are born "defective," is telling, in that it forces us to acknowledge the damage we already tacitly accept for the sake of modern civilization (Kahn 2007, 46). But his comments are also cold, based on numbers and data rather than the lived experience of, in this case, parenting. They have the effect of turning *man (and woman) into numbers*.

The situation these six survivors now find themselves in is, for some at least, intolerable in its uncertainty, and belies the confidence about the adaptability of humans expressed by Strangelove and before him by Kahn. As survivor-doctor Jane explains:

> if we live together and radiation is sufficiently high, we risk one of two things. The first is sterility, and that would be disastrous psychologically. The second is we might produce monsters, terrible mutations who bear no resemblance to human beings. Of course, if radiation isn't high, we might have perfectly normal children. We might in time create an oasis of life in the middle of a desert of death. But we won't know until perhaps it's too late.
>
> (George 1965, 139)

George takes the opportunity of the survivor's conversation to interpolate a good amount of criticism of the Arms Race and the ludicrous situation of being able to destroy humanity many times over (George 1965, 132–36). But it is this uncertainty about the survivor's most basic desires (and as survivors their most basic responsibilities) that rams home George's critique of the abstract theorizing of strategists like Kahn. Jane tries to use reasoned calculation, but that rhetoric is now subsumed within their very human and tragic situation. That tragedy plays itself out in their responses, especially when it appears that a mother chimpanzee has given birth to a hideously deformed infant (George 1965, 186). Jane and fellow survivor Bill have already decided to live together by this point, and the pregnant Jane first suffers a miscarriage in shock at the deformed infant chimpanzee and then commits suicide in despair.

It would appear that some survivors do envy the dead, and Bill (who is covertly given many markers associating him with the author) follows his love and shoots himself (George 1965, 190–91).[16] As the remaining four dig shallow graves to bury their colleagues and friends they hit the metal of one of the silos which have been filled with supplies for the surviving elect planned before the war. Unlike the scenario of *Dr. Strangelove*, the U.S. authorities this time have had time to act on Kahn's advice and to prepare for a post-war environment. What readers of *Commander-1* are soon to discover is that these silos are not simply filled with food supplies, they (there are a number of them, just as there are a number of islands) are stockpiled with weapons and also contain sperm banks. The irony of the survivors burying Jane and Bill on the top of silos filled with frozen human sperm, the freezing made possible by the limitless power supplied by nuclear generators, is fierce. But it is also wholly appropriate. George's novel is fast becoming one about the end of civil society, and in a very genuine sense the end of humanity.

Interspersed with the events on the island, the novel presents us with Geraghty's return to Safe Base One and his quick rise (everyone else of comparative rank being dead or dying) to the top of the military hierarchy. Geraghty has no doubts that the military, under his command, must return to the islands, open up the silos, enforce a strict regime, and restart humanity on a more secure footing. He is faced on Safe Base One by a civilian revolt, headed by ex-Senator Brecht, who tries to preserve the ideas of elected office and civic society. Geraghty brutally crushes the resistance, institutes a program of indoctrination (which includes drugging people into subservience) and rather chillingly explains, in rhetoric best described as Orwellian: "We're still at war because we're fighting for the future. We're fighting not for ourselves, but for the human race" (George 1965, 173). But this is a human race that is white, obscenely patriarchal, fascist in the precise sense that it seeks to eliminate all difference, and has learnt nothing from the global apocalypse save how easily defeated ideas of democracy are in the context of a nuclear holocaust.

The island havens, safe from the effects of radiation, are the ideological offspring of Strangelove's and Kahn's mineshafts. They are a fascist utopia (a humanistic dystopia), and they offer Geraghty and those immediately under his command the chance of "a new World" order (George 1965, 197). George does not miss his opportunity to point out the role played by nuclear power in this story.[17] In a passage clearly linked to Strangelove's nightmare visions of a new world for a selected few, Geraghty considers the power ("sixteen Polaris missiles," "the jeeps, the guns, the fuel, and the food," along with "huge sperm banks") that nuclear energy has given him: "He thought what a blessing nuclear reactors had proved to be [. . .] So he had available an unlimited source of power. In fact, he had power, period" (George 1965, 217).

In the series of texts (novels, films, treatise, and treatments) with which we are dealing, the connection between nuclear and political power has never been made so explicitly. Kahn's censure of all those who take an apocalyptic approach to nuclear weapons has been proven correct: an all-out nuclear (and it turns out chemical) war has not led to total annihilation, rather it has led to an irresistible world dictatorship. One wonders at first why Geraghty and the now defunct administration thought it necessary to stockpile so many nuclear weapons. We only have to listen to what Geraghty says; even in a situation of near annihilation where only just upwards of 10,000 U.S. citizens of the right color survive on the islands and roughly 100,000 defenseless remnants in the world, the utility of such weapons is not in their usability but in the power they help generate and underpin.

Once on the island, with women reduced to "selected future leader breeders," the scale and sheer horror of Geraghty's plans begin to be manifest. He is clearly taking the opportunity that the survival operation, and his chance elevation, have given him, to establish his own peculiarly sexless, narcissistic brand of fascism. His explanation about his plans to eventually recolonize all inhabitable land and, in the process, eliminate all surviving indigenous populations, is truly shocking. As he puts it to the remaining male "guinea pigs" Arnie and John (he doesn't feel the need to explain anything to Helen and Mary): "We've had this racial problem once before in the world, but this time we can make sure we don't have it again" (George 1965, 250).

The most telling point about Geraghty, and perhaps the most strikingly achieved aspect of George's surprisingly undervalued novel, is that the Commander is not a sci-fi monster. Neither is he a Dr. Strangelove producing laughter because of his hilarious ("mad") contributions to a "nightmare comedy." He is a character that readers should remember they started by identifying and finding some empathy with. Geraghty is a brilliant study in the essentially narcissistic nature of fascism as a politics and a psychology (it is that tendency within humans to want to eliminate alterity itself). He is not a stage monster because he is so plausible and familiar; and in that he is all the more terrifying.

As the last four "guinea pigs" attempt to escape the nightmare of the island and Geraghty's regime they are gunned down and with their deaths are lost the last examples of free humanity. Ironically, we might observe, they were the last humans *not* to be guinea pigs. The date of this arrival of total "blackness" is significantly December 25, 1966 (George 1965, 253).

It has taken only one year to eliminate all chances of resistance. George did in fact write one further section, unpublished in the 1965 edition. Here we return to Geraghty's Journal where he triumphs in the elimination of the four survivors and his achievements in establishing his brave new, "clean" dictatorship.[18]

Commander-1 is a fascinating and truly undervalued development of many of the serious implications within Kubrick's famous film and the Strangelove project more widely. In particular, it takes that film's hints about the U.S. military industrial complex and fascism and explores and explains it in great and compelling depth. Linking Kubrick and George through their collective responses to Kahn helps demonstrate just how significant and powerful was their approach to the link between *the delicate balance of terror* and the *delicate balance between democracy and dictatorship*. It also clarifies how shockingly relevant Kubrick's "nightmare comedy" is to our current political circumstances. If it seems frightening how easily we might slip into nuclear conflict, then it should be just as frightening how easy it can be to slip from elected to unelected, military rule. Given recent events it is a point that we need more than ever to place at the front of our minds.

Notes

1 Readers might compare and contrast my account of the politics of Peter George's work here to the rather different conclusion drawn by Peter Krämer (2013).
2 In an interview published on February 22, 1964, George said of his new novel: "This is not science fiction. This is what could happen. This is what is presently possible." See the Stanley Kubrick Archive, University of London Arts: SK/11/6/18–19.
3 See notes for "The Rise of Doctor Strangelove" in SK/11/1/16, where an interviewer states: "Doctor Strangelove you have been referred to in the press, in connection with your book, as a monster, an inhuman, dangerous man, a crack pot realist and so forth."
4 For the former see, for example, references to the description of the game of "Chicken" (which Kahn takes from Bertram Russell in 2007, 291) in Kubrick's hand in loose notes in SK/11/1/12. Examples of the latter come in numerous places (such as a typed text SK/11/1/11 date March 22, 1962) and can be said to channel into the various versions of the U.S. President's summative speeches which were finally edited out of the film version (see the "Serious Version" of July 23, 1962: SK/11/14).
5 For Kahn's strong objection to being associated with the term see Broderick, 189, n.42.
6 This discussion leads Kahn to consider swapping cities as a military and political option, an idea we can find in George's novel two years earlier and throughout the various scripts and treatments associated with the Strangelove project.
7 See OTW: 79–80, 85, 88.
8 This title is previously mentioned in a *Dr. Strangelove* script dated January 1, 1963, SK/11/1/23.

9 George adopts this from a script that has no date but seems connected to the scripts dated January 1, 1963, SK/11/1/24.
10 George is drawing on versions of the President's speech found in many places in the archive, including: SK/11/1/14; SK/11/1/20; SK/11/1/21; SK/11/1/24.
11 For further references to world government, see Kahn 2007, 494, 527.
12 It is worth noting here that George had originally entertained the title "Nucleus of Survivors" for the title of his novel. See Broderick. 161, n.119. See also SK/11/6/18–19.
13 See "Some Notes on the Character of Strangelove including Strangelove's Theory" in George 2015, 183–214. See also SK/11/1/22.
14 George no doubt has China's shock testing of an A bomb in 1964 in mind.
15 Kahn makes much of the utility of cheap radiation meters distributed to as many U.S. citizens as possible. Kahn 2007, 85–86, 111–12.
16 Some of these markers include using the name of his son, David, for the son of the New York couple at the beginning of the novel (see, 6–7). Bill is a Welshman who shares his hometown, Treorchy, with Peter George (see, 82). On the question of whether Bill's suicide predicts Peter George's own suicide in 1966, see the quotation from Sara George in Broderick, 18.
17 In the interview found in SK/11/6/18–19, George makes it clear that he is for "universal [nuclear] disarmament of all kinds."
18 MS transcript provided courtesy of David George. The text forms part of a two-part supplement to Geraghty's Journal. It is not clear why it was cut from the final edit of the novel, and there is a possibility this editorial cut was not sanctioned by George himself. Information from an email by David George to me sent in July 2016.

Works cited

Aligica, Paul Dragos, and Kenneth R. Weinstein. 2009. "Herman Kahn: A Bio-Bibliographical Note." In *The Essential Herman Kahn: In Defense of Thinking*, edited by Paul Dragos Aligica and Kenneth R. Weinstein, 267–74. Plymouth: Rowan and Littlefield Pubs.

Broderick, Mick. 2017. *Reconstructing Strangelove: Inside Stanley Kubrick's 'Nightmare Comedy'*. London and New York: Wallflower Press.

Clarke, Arthur C. 1968. *2001: A Space Odyssey*. London: Orbit.

Cordle, Daniel. 2008. *States of Suspense: The Nuclear Age, Postmodernism and United States Fiction and Prose*. Manchester and New York: Manchester University Press.

Daniels, Richard. 2017. "The Stanley Kubrick Archive: A Filmmaker's Legacy." *Screening the Past*, no. 42. *Dossier: Post-Kubrick*, edited by Mick Broderick. www.screening.the past.com/issue-42. Accessed November 30, 2017.

George, Peter [Peter Bryant]. 1958. *Red Alert*. Rockville, MD: Black Mask Books.

———. 1965. *Commander-1*. London: Heinemann.

———. 2015. *Dr. Strangelove or: How I Learned to Stop Worrying and Love the Bomb*. Cardiff: Candy Jar Press.

Ghamari-Tabrizi, Sharon. 2005. *The Worlds of Herman Kahn: The Intuitive Science of Thermonuclear War*. Cambridge, MA: Harvard University Press.

Kahn, Herman. 1962. *Thinking About the Unthinkable*. New York: Avon Books.
———. 2007. *On Thermonuclear War*. New Brunswick, NJ and London: Transactions Publishers.
Kaplan, Fred. 1983. *The Wizards of Armageddon*. Stanford, CA: Stanford University Press.
Kolker, Robert. 2011. *A Cinema of Loneliness*. 4th ed. Oxford and New York: Oxford University Press.
Krämer, Peter. 2010. *2001: A Space Odyssey* (BFI Film Classics). London: Palgrave Macmillan.
———. 2013. "'The Greatest Mass Murderer Since Adolf Hitler': Nuclear War and the Nazi Past in *Dr. Strangelove*." In *Dramatising Disaster: Character, Event, Representation*, edited by Christine Cornea and Rhys Owain Thomas, 120–35. Cambridge: Cambridge Scholars Publishing.
———. 2014. *Dr. Strangelove or: How I Learned to Stop Worrying and Love the Bomb* (BFI Film Classics). London: Palgrave Macmillan.
Kubrick, Stanley. 1964. *Dr. Strangelove or: How I Learned to Stop Worrying and Love the Bomb*. Columbia Pictures.

4 Looking back, looking ahead
Kubrick and music

Christine Gengaro

Director Martin Scorsese once said: "We're all the children of D.W. Griffith and Stanley Kubrick" (quoted in Kolker 2015, 75). While it is likely he was referring specifically to visual film language, there is also something to be said about the musical legacies of these filmmakers. In the case of Kubrick, the musical choices he made for his films throughout his career point to an interesting evolution, one that has influenced numerous filmmakers. The use of music in Kubrick's films seems to point to a development that, little by little, moved away from the traditional model (hiring someone to score the edited film) to an autonomous process of choosing pre-existent music for his films—thus avoiding creative conflicts with composers. Of course, both of these models of Kubrick's artistic journey are grossly oversimplified, and like any true evolution, eschewed the path of a straight line in favor of far more interesting twists and turns. This aim of this chapter is four-fold: (1) contextualize Kubrick's musical choices as part of film music history; (2) chart his own personal development through different modes of scoring; (3) discuss *2001: A Space Odyssey* specifically as an artistic, financial, and aesthetic turning point; and (4) look at contemporary directors who have been influenced by Kubrick's style.

The development of film music

Starting with *2001: A Space Odyssey* (1968) and subsequently with *A Clockwork Orange* (1971), *Barry Lyndon* (1975), and *The Shining* (1980), Kubrick began to privilege classical music or art music (music from a cultivated tradition with structural and notational concerns; both terms imply inclusion in the Western canon) in film as an acceptable and desirable option for a score. Although it may have seemed to some that this was groundbreaking, using pre-existent music—especially art music—for film was, in fact, a return to earlier practices.

In the early days of silent film, a musical score was frequently improvised by a cinema pianist (Cooke 2008, 12). The score of a film could therefore vary widely from theater to theater, depending on the skill of the cinema pianist and his grasp of the emotional content of the film. Pianists might have also used fragments of well-known tunes in their repertoire, and over time, certain pieces came to have accepted meanings for actions on screen. After 1910, collections of musical choices for specific films began to emerge. Such collections could be arrangements for the solo pianist or adapted for ensembles, and they might be a mix of newly composed material and preexistent music (Hickman 2006, 67). By the 1920s, some clever editors put together collections to aid the cinema pianist in the selections of appropriate musical themes (Cooke 2008, 16). Musical anthologies such as Ernö Rapée's *Motion Picture Moods for Pianists and Organists* (1924) and *Encyclopedia of Music for Pictures* (1925) provided quick reference—organized by mood or event—for the working cinema musician. Collections such as these contained excerpts of the work of Mozart, Brahms, Wagner, and many others, and formed many of the musical "clichés that remain firmly in the popular imagination" (Cooke 2008, 16).

As the popularity of film grew, and the art of filmmaking developed, musical accompaniment changed as well. Larger theaters employed bigger ensembles, and the scores had to be planned out meticulously for multi-reel films and larger playing groups. Theaters hired music directors whose duties included "arranging and conducting appropriate repertoire drawn either from the classical extracts or short original pieces published in anthologies, from cue sheets, or preparing freshly selected passages" (Cooke 2008, 20). A "cue sheet" was a list of musical suggestions for specific scenes that was sent to the theater with a film. The Edison Film Company, for example, began using cue sheets as a way to exert a modicum of control over the musical accompaniment (and one might argue the emotional content) of their films (Hickman 2006, 68). A large epic film like D.W. Griffith's *Birth of a Nation* (1915) began with a score entirely compiled by Carli Elinor from excerpts of Mozart, Rossini, Wagner, and others, but was then given some original cues by a composer, in this case Joseph Carl Breil. The resultant score was a hybrid of new cues, pre-existent classical music, and Civil War-era tunes. After the emergence of sound film in 1927, Breil's score for *Birth of a Nation* was synchronized and recorded with the film, thus popularizing the idea of a bespoke score, especially for large films with complex narratives (Cooke 2008, 24–25). Subsequently, more and more directors called upon composers to write new scores specifically designed for their films. The use of pre-existent classical music as score began to fall out of favor, but such cues never left entirely, providing other functions within film narrative.

Looking back, looking ahead 39

In the 1950s, the "pop score" emerged. In certain kinds of films (especially those marketed to youth culture), the big orchestral score began to lose traction, and filmmakers saw the artistic possibilities—and the immense potential profits—of compiling and selling a soundtrack full of popular songs (Cooke 2008, 274). We can trace this practice back to the rock songs of *The Blackboard Jungle* (1955) and the soundtracks to *Jailhouse Rock* (1957) and other Elvis Presley films; these pop and rock soundtracks came to dominate films of the late 1960s such as *Easy Rider* (1969) and *Midnight Cowboy* (1969). The soundtrack album itself became a commodity and an additional income generator for producers and studios. All of Kubrick's films from 1968 on used pre-existent music to varying degrees. Some, like *Full Metal Jacket* (1987), fit into the mold of the pop score, while others, like *2001: A Space Odyssey* and *The Shining* (1980), used art music for nearly every musical cue. The next section explores Kubrick's scores through the years and considers the musical trends apparent in his artistic development.

Kubrick's musical scores

The scores of Kubrick's films defy easy categorization. Many of them use multiple modes of scoring including the use of newly composed pieces, arrangements of pre-existent music (both pop and classical), and recordings of pre-existent art and pop music. If we attempt to find the common threads among the scores, there are many, but five main categories point to Kubrick's most distinctive scoring choices.

The most coherent category consists of films with primarily a newly written score: *Day of the Fight* (short) (1951), *The Flying Padre* (short) (1951), *Fear and Desire* (1953), *Killer's Kiss* (1955), *The Killing* (1956), *Paths of Glory* (1957), and *Spartacus* (1960). Composer Gerald Fried wrote the music for all of these films with the exception of *The Flying Padre*, scored by Nathaniel Shillkret, and *Spartacus*, which was the work of Alex North. Fried and Kubrick knew each other having grown up in the same Bronx neighborhood. When Kubrick needed music for his first short film, he asked Fried. The composer surmised that he was chosen because he was the only musician with whom Kubrick was acquainted.

As one might expect, Fried and North composed music using Kubrick's shot footage, thereby tailoring their work to the narrative and emotional needs of the film. Kubrick had varying levels of input on this process according to an interview Gerald Fried gave to Karen Herman at the Archive of American Television in 2003. At the beginning of their collaboration, Fried noted that he was free to do what he felt was best for the first two films with minimal comment from the director. In the interview, Fried also mentioned that this began to change in their third collaboration, *Killer's Kiss*. By then,

Fried says, "we were already arguing. The fourth and fifth score, there were knockdown battles. But by that time, [Kubrick] had developed a taste and a style and he was a hard guy to argue with [. . .] At the beginning, it was easy, I went my own way, but by [. . .] *Paths of Glory*, I had to justify every note" (2003).

Alex North was already attached to *Spartacus* by the time Kubrick replaced original director Anthony Mann. Even though North wasn't hired by Kubrick, the two seemed to work well together. In North's biography, their professional relationship is characterized as having "a deep, mutual understanding" (Henderson 1993, 71). Since the production of *Spartacus* took place over many months, North was able to assemble temporary tracks of his new compositions to give Kubrick a sense of the musical score as it was being written. Kubrick was comfortable asking North to add music in places where he felt cues were necessary, providing the composer with a list of suggestions near the end of production. The final score had more than 70 musical cues and covered more than two-thirds of the three-hour-and-17-minute run time. Many critics agree that the score served the film well, and it was nominated for several awards, including an Oscar.

A second significant category of Kubrick's scoring techniques involves films for which there is a pre-existent song used as an emotional or narrational touchstone. In this category, we may include *Killer's Kiss*, *Dr. Strangelove*, *Lolita*, and *Barry Lyndon*. In *Killer's Kiss*, Kubrick chose "Once" by Norman Gimbel and Arden Clar for Gerald Fried to incorporate into the score. In addition to all of the new cues Fried composed, there are numerous arrangements of this song that appear in different contexts. In a club, the swing band arrangement of the song is shown on screen as diegetic; an orchestral version of it provides underscore for some scenes; a version with violin soloist evokes longing; a slow, jazzy version with trombone soloist accompanies some dancers. The tune in its many guises evokes different moods, and yet its ubiquity seems to echo the centrality of the love story, continually reminding us of the protagonists' struggle and their desire for connection.

For *Lolita*, Kubrick's producing partner James Harris suggested they use music (untitled at the time) composed by his brother Bob as the love theme for the film. Notable film composer and Hitchcock collaborator, Bernard Herrmann, refused an offer to work on the project because of Kubrick's insistence that the song be part of the score (LoBrutto 1999, 214). Herrmann would not arrange someone else's song, and was in fact a vociferous critic of using pre-existent music in film. Kubrick made an interesting choice thereafter—he hired bandleader and arranger Nelson Riddle, who willingly used the pre-existent song. He was also given the opportunity to write a few short cues of his own, and was amenable to accepting Kubrick's requested changes (Levinson 2001, 206). The opening of the film features a lushly orchestrated version of Bob Harris' "love theme" accompanying a long take of Humbert's hands painting Lolita's toenails. It re-appears when Lolita bids a sad farewell to Humbert as she leaves for summer camp, and it returns when Lolita and Humbert move to Beardsley College. It is heard twice more: once when Humbert realizes that Lolita has found a way to escape from him, and then in the final scenes as Humbert attempts to convince Lolita to leave her husband. This cue continues with variations into the final credits. There is also a pop song touchstone in *Lolita*; "Lolita Ya-Ya" was composed by Bob Harris and Nelson Riddle. Actress Sue Lyon provided the vocals for the song and also for the B-side, "Turn Off the Moon." "Lolita Ya-Ya," which appears when Humbert first sees Lolita, may be interpreted as the musical representation of the flirtation between them, while the love theme represents Humbert's unnatural idealization of Lolita (Schultheis 2007, 268).

Kubrick's subsequent film *Dr. Strangelove* was scored by British bandleader and arranger, Laurie Johnson. Johnson's primary contribution to the film consisted of eight different arrangements of "When Johnny Comes Marching Home" during the B-52 scenes. Some variations play through the entirety of the tune, while others feature just phrases. The instrumentation and tempo shift from variation to variation, but a snare drum is present in all of them. There are also notable pre-existing tunes that bookend the film. The romantic "Try a Little Tenderness" appears during the opening credits. The final cue is the iconic World War II-era song made famous by Vera Lynn, "We'll Meet Again." This song provides ironic counterpoint to the chain reaction of bombs that detonate and destroy mankind. The bulk of *Dr. Strangelove* has no musical underscore, especially in the war room scenes, allowing the ironic and comedic dialogue to take center-stage.

One of the films that benefits the most from the repeated use of a musical cue is *Barry Lyndon*. For this film, Kubrick hired Leonard Rosenman, who acted as arranger for many of the pre-existent pieces that are on the score (Gengaro 2012, 151). G.F. Handel's *Sarabande* from his Keyboard Suite in D minor appears ten times in ten distinct arrangements throughout the film, totaling more than 30 minutes of screen time. It accompanies everything from duels to a quiet card game to a funeral. The original work is short—just 16 measures, but Rosenman used changing instrumentation and subtle shifts in tempo to effectively create different moods (Gengaro 2012, 155–57).

One may also argue that the use of Richard Strauss' *Also Sprach Zarathustra* in *2001: A Space Odyssey* also fits into this category, as a piece that appears a few times throughout the course of a film to great effect. It opens the film and appears at the end as well. It also accompanies the iconic scene of the proto-human ape—having touched the mysterious monolith—discovering that a bone can become a weapon.

The third category includes film scores that mix both pre-existent classical music with popular music: *A Clockwork Orange*, *Barry Lyndon*, *The Shining*, and *Eyes Wide Shut*. The score for *A Clockwork Orange* consists primarily of pre-existent works by Beethoven, Rossini, Purcell, and Elgar, some of which were played or "realized" on a Moog synthesizer by Wendy Carlos, while some are simply recordings. In addition, there are two songs of a more popular style: "I Want to Marry a Lighthouse Keeper," by Erika Eigen and "Overture to the Sun" by Terry Tucker. *Barry Lyndon* uses mostly period-appropriate popular and folk music for the score as well as work by Mozart, Handel, and Schubert (for more on musical anachronism in *Barry Lyndon*, see Lash 2017, 83–93). Kubrick also chose some recordings by Irish performing groups for scenes depicting Redmond Barry's youth in Ireland, and made use of military songs during sequences showing his time in the British service.

The Shining, which has a score replete with avant-garde art music, also makes use of 1930s popular songs such as "Midnight, the Stars, and You" and "It's All Forgotten Now." For this film Kubrick employs the music of Krzysztof Penderecki, György Ligeti, and Béla Bartók seemingly to represent Jack's gradual descent into madness, while the popular tunes provide a seductive veneer that draws him further into the grasp of the Hotel. Kubrick's final film, *Eyes Wide Shut*, famously features a waltz by Shostakovich, a haunting piano piece by Ligeti, and popular songs, some of which provide ironic commentary such as "Strangers in the Night" to accompany Bill's conversation with a masked woman, and "I Want a Boy for Christmas," which plays as Bill searches for his friend Nick.

The fourth category includes films that primarily employ "borrowed music" (either pop or classical) with a few newly composed cues. In *A Clockwork Orange*, Kubrick uses an excerpt of just one wholly original piece, "Timesteps" by Wendy Carlos, within the borrowed music score. For *The Shining*, Wendy Carlos also contributed the cues "Rocky Mountains" and "Shining/Heartbeat" (Carlos' most prominent contribution to the score is the Moog arrangement of the *Dies Irae* chant heard over the opening credits). For *Full Metal Jacket*, Kubrick chose a number of rock songs from the era for the soundtrack, but scores a climactic scene with some haunting original music by his daughter Vivian Kubrick (credited as Abigail Mead). Jocelyn Pook contributed four cues to *Eyes Wide Shut* including the eerie "Masked Ball," which is played at the strange party at which the protagonist finds himself (this piece is actually a reworking of a tune Pook had written previously known as "Backwards Priests," see Gengaro 2012, 236–37). Although it is possible to parse and categorize Kubrick's scores in different ways, the final category should acknowledge Kubrick's privileging of pre-existent classical or art music in certain scores. The most obvious example of this is *2001: A Space Odyssey*, which is something of an anomaly in Kubrick's oeuvre as it is the only Kubrick film with a score entirely made up of pre-existent art music. (Three non-classical cues appear sourced on screen.) Although Kubrick is considered a pioneer in the modern use of pre-existent classical music over newly written scores, his musical choices were always more nuanced, as evidenced by the categories mentioned above. Similarly, while Kubrick's other films mix modes of scoring, films that apply classical music forms as the primary voice on the score include: *Barry Lyndon*, *A Clockwork Orange*, *The Shining*, and, arguably, *Eyes Wide Shut*. Perhaps Kubrick's most exceptional work in this regard is *2001: A Space Odyssey* because it embodies a significant shift in the writer-director-producer's style, and it stands out from the other films in this category because it is the first, and demonstrably the most influential.

The shift of *2001: A Space Odyssey*

The use of pre-existent music in *2001: A Space Odyssey* may have seemed to some like a surprising creative deviation, but if we look at his two preceding films, we can observe Kubrick already turning away from using newly written scores. *Lolita* and *Dr. Strangelove* employed arrangers at the musical helm, better to shape versions of the music Kubrick had chosen for the projects. Whether or not this was his intention, using Riddle and Johnson primarily as arrangers allowed Kubrick to avoid conflict with composers whose creative impulses might have gone against his. By the time he began work on *2001* it seems that Kubrick had already intended to use all pre-existent music on the soundtrack (Agel 1970, 198; Merkley 2007, 21). And yet, composer Alex North was hired to write an original score, either at the behest of MGM executives, who insisted that a project of that scope needed an original score, or by Kubrick himself, who perhaps wanted the option of new music (Merkley 2007, 21). For many years, it was assumed that the temporary tracks Kubrick used for rough cuts during production (most likely to show to executives) became so attached to the footage that Kubrick couldn't let them go, but it seems that that was not the case.

In an interview with author Tony Thomas, composer Jerry Goldsmith—who ended up conducting North's "lost" *2001* score for a 1993 recording—said "it is a mistake to force music into a film, and for me *2001* was ruined by Kubrick's choice of music. His selections had no relationship, and the pieces could not comment on the film because they were not part of it [...] A score is a fabric which must be tailored to the film" (1979, 228). Kubrick's choice, however, was supported by the financial success of the soundtrack. The initial release sold so well that MGM released a second album featuring, as it says on the cover, "Music Inspired by MGM's Presentation of the Stanley Kubrick Production" (MGM 1968). Other than Richard Strauss' opening to the tone poem, *Also Sprach Zarathustra*, there is no other music from the film on this album. Instead, we find a curated collection of cuts that are similar in character to the cues in the film, including *Lontano* and *Volumina* by Ligeti, and Richard Strauss' Waltzes from *Der Rosenkavalier*. Seeing a valuable opportunity for selling music in this repertoire, CBS released their own album called *Selections from 2001* that featured recordings of pieces used in the film performed by the Philadelphia Orchestra and the New York Philharmonic.

Taking into account both North's unused score and the pre-existent choices for *2001: A Space Odyssey*, film critic Roger Ebert suggested that North's score would have subverted Kubrick's aim, which as Ebert saw it was to inspire contemplation rather than emotion. "The classical music chosen by Kubrick exists *outside* the action. It uplifts. It wants to be sublime; it brings a seriousness and transcendence to the visuals" (Ebert 1997). Ebert adds that Kubrick's use of the chosen music avoids a pitfall of using recognizable classical music cues, namely trivialization. Rather, *2001* achieves something special in that it is "almost unique in *enhancing* the music by its association with his images" (Ebert 1997). Blogger Dominick Moreira sees this as almost the opposite of what most directors do: "Rather than adding tracks to fill in some sort of atmosphere within the scene, he uses music to create many scenes" (2016). Likewise, composer and sound designer Paul Charlier views Kubrick's choices in the bigger picture: "free[ing] directors from the mould of how music, especially orchestral music, was composed, produced, and incorporated within film" (quoted in Byrnes 2013). Journalist Paul Byrnes agreed, stating: "In effect, [Kubrick] helped reduce the hegemony of the big orchestral scores that had so dominated the 1930s and 1940s [...] For a while after *2001*, those big scores were less dominant until John Williams came along with *Star Wars*" (2013).

Alex North's reaction to the borrowed music score of *2001: A Space Odyssey* was utter surprise. He hadn't been told about the final scoring decisions and watched at the premiere as the film ran with none of his cues. Kubrick was perhaps a bit cagey with North (Merkley 2007; Heimerdinger 2011; Gengaro 2012), suggesting to the composer that he might mix both the newly written cues with the classical recordings. However, after the success of *2001* and its soundtrack, it seems that Kubrick was much more transparent about what he wanted for the music of his films. He had nothing to hide; he proved himself to be in a league of his own by that point. In his future endeavors Kubrick seemed to make it clear to everyone involved—composers, arrangers, music supervisors, and support staff who did musical research for him—that he wanted options. He would be the one making the final choices, and many selections (perhaps all) would go unchosen.

The financial success of the soundtrack albums could only have provided encouragement and validation for Kubrick. The score of *2001: A Space Odyssey*, despite its age, still surprises and delights, and many of Kubrick's choices for the film have entered into cultural consciousness, inspiring both imitation and parody. In fact, spotting Kubrick references has become something of a hobby for fans. An ever-growing crowd-sourced list of all pop culture references to this film exists at wikia.com. There are many musical references included, like the use of Richard Strauss's *Also Sprach Zarathustra* in an early episode of *The Simpsons* and "Daisy Bell" in a series 7 episode of *Doctor Who*. The visual and aural language of Kubrick, and of this film in particular, have influenced countless filmmakers (Broderick 2017). And although it may seem to some that Kubrick's use of classical music in film was a revolutionary gesture—certainly in the genre of science fiction, it was, in fact, a reprise of a common practice used in film at the very genesis of the art form.

The Kubrick effect

Kubrick's choices were very influential in the realm of classical music and film, but also in the sense of curating pre-existent selections to fit a film. In colloquial parlance, we may term this collection a mixtape or playlist. When Kubrick chose the score of *2001*, he made a conscious decision to use not just those pieces, but those *specific* recordings that he'd used in editing. Since Kubrick's artistic success with *2001: A Space Odyssey*, and with the financial profits made by the soundtrack album, using pre-existent classical music in film gained a kind of cultural cachet. There are filmmakers working today whose choices have mimicked Kubrick's methods. Additionally, buying the rights to recordings is sometimes less expensive than hiring both a composer to write an original score and an entire orchestra to record it, so using pre-existent music can be an economical practice as well as an artistic choice.

Preparing a score from pre-existent sources could also be very attractive to directors who are searching for the right chemistry with their collaborators. There's a well-known story about George Lucas—who was keeping Kubrick's *2001: A Space Odyssey* in mind—wanting to score *Star Wars* with pre-existent choices like Gustav Holst's *The Planets* and film music by composer Erich Wolfgang Korngold. Lucas' friend Steven Spielberg recommended he speak with John Williams before committing to using the classical music. At this point, Williams had collaborated with Spielberg on *The Sugarland Express* (1974) and *Jaws* (1975) and would go on to write the scores to all but a handful of Spielberg's films. Williams heard the pieces Lucas wanted for the score and believed he could deliver something similar, but still original and tailor-made for the film. This was similar to the arrangement ostensibly struck between North and Kubrick. North heard all of Kubrick's temp-track choices and attempted to write music with similar tempos, accents, and instrumentation (see Jon Burlingame's liner notes to *Music for 2001: A Space Odyssey: The Original Score*, 2007, Intrada Special Collection). Although Kubrick ultimately rejected North's work, Lucas used Williams's music. And of course, in retrospect, no one can imagine anything other than the score Williams delivered, which served the film (and its subsequent sequels and prequels) admirably. But this is due in no small measure to Williams' considerable aptitude for finding something new to say in a familiar language. Music critic and columnist for the *New Yorker*, Alex Ross, sees Williams' unique talent as saying "I can mimic anything you want, but you need a living voice" (*The New Yorker* January 1, 2016).

There are historical and dramatic implications in the use of pre-existent music in film, but this seems to be a far greater concern for musicologists and film scholars than it was for Kubrick, at least to the extent that he would admit. When asked why he chose art music that had already been written, already possessing its own history, function, and meaning, Kubrick said: "I don't see any reason not to avail yourself of the great orchestral music of the past and present" (Ciment 1999, 153). Interestingly, in reference to the compiled score for *Birth of a Nation*, composer and music director Carli Elinor's similar opinion seemed to support the idea that "there was no need for original music since so many good tunes had already been written" (Darby and DuBois 1990, 3).

Kubrick's musical choices were, of course, much more deliberate and self-conscious than those of Griffith, but they speak to the half a century of film history that separates these directors. Kubrick's musical methods in *2001*, *A Clockwork Orange*, *Barry Lyndon*, *The Shining*, *Full Metal Jacket*, and *Eyes Wide Shut* are all masterclasses in how to use pre-existent music. That is not to say that this move towards pre-existent scores would not have happened without Kubrick, but the soundtrack to *2001: A Space Odyssey* was such a staggeringly successful gamble, it made pre-existent classical music a valid scoring choice for up-and-coming directors.

We can find examples of pre-existent music in many films, even in films by directors who are the staunchest users of newly written scores. But there are some directors working today who have shown a unique penchant for using pre-existent music. Three directors come to mind whose use of pre-existent music outweighs their use of newly written score: Tarantino, Scorsese, and Malick.

Quentin Tarantino has famously said that he uses music from his own collection when he's writing a screenplay (Marshall 2014). For him, choosing music comes either before—or at the same time—as the creation of the film. Tarantino's early film scores relied primarily on popular music cues, but he has gradually expanded his methods, using some newly composed cues and also excerpts from older film scores. *Django Unchained* (2012), for example, featured cues from Ennio Morricone's scores for *Two Mules for Sister Sara* (1970) and *The Hellbenders* (also known as *The Cruel Ones*, 1967). Tarantino's *The Hateful Eight* (2015) is actually the very first among his films to use primarily newly written score. Ennio Morricone, who won both Academy Award and Golden Globe for the score, composed over 50 minutes of new music for the film.

Martin Scorsese has been one of the greatest champions of using pre-existent music in his films. Many of his selections have been popular songs, but he has also made great use of classical music, specifically but not exclusively Italian Romantic opera. The uses are both diegetic and non-diegetic, and at times, the plot of the opera or even the content of an aria might provide commentary on the scene. For example, the aria "Nessun Dorma" from Giacomo Puccini's *Turandot* seems to have narrative significance in Scorsese's segment "Life Lessons" from *New York Stories* (1989). Some of Scorsese's characters attend an opera, like Jack Nicholson's mob boss in *The Departed* (2006) seeing Gaetano Donizetti's tragedy *Lucia di Lammermoor*, or the main characters attending Charles Gounod's *Faust* in *The Age of Innocence* (1993). One of Scorsese's best-known opening gambits is the use of the Intermezzo from Pietro Mascagni's 1890 opera *Cavalleria Rusticana* for the opening sequence of *Raging Bull* (1980). The peaceful music in the opera provides a brief moment of calm before the tragic duel between Alfio and Turiddu, while Scorsese uses it to introduce us to Jake LaMotta, who prowls the ring in slow motion, bouncing and punching the air in a sequence that feels more like ballet than boxing. There are also interesting musical choices in *Casino* (1995), including the opening credit sequence scored with the *St. Matthew Passion*, J.S. Bach's oratorio about the Biblical Passion story. In the blog Den of Geek, Glen Chapman noted that the score for *Casino* fits perfectly into Scorsese's style: "a brilliant mix tape that includes a mixture of familiar and lesser known tracks" (2010).

The score to Scorsese's *Shutter Island* (2010) was something of a departure, since many of the selections were dissonant and instrumental. The intriguing score owes a great deal to Scorsese's collaboration with music supervisor, Robbie Robertson, who has worked with Scorsese on the scores of a few films, and notably, one of Scorsese's early projects was the documentary, *The Last Waltz* (1978), about Robertson's band, The Band. Robertson read the script for *Shutter Island* and reasoned that certain pre-existent pieces could help Scorsese achieve his dramatic aims: "In the back of my mind was the thought, why don't we have some geniuses who could really amplify the emotional ideas" (quoted in Swed 2010). Of the soundtrack, critic Mark Swed noted that "the music doesn't cue the action or explain anything. It adds emotional texture, serving as an alternate universe for a film that has at its essence an alternate universe" (2010). It was such a bold choice of twentieth-century composers—including John Cage, Morton Feldman, and György Ligeti (a favorite of Kubrick), among others—that even Scorsese wondered if they were too far out for the project. Trusting in Robertson and his own musical sophistication, Scorsese used the choices to great effect. Among the selections are Ligeti's *Lontano*, which Kubrick used in *The Shining*, and selections from Penderecki, whose music provided so much of the soundscape of that film.

Currently, we may view the continuing use of pre-existent classical music in film as having varying degrees of depth and meaning. The majority of instances of classical music in film act simply as set dressing, much as furniture or a clothing style might give you hints about time or place, or elements of a character's personality. Less frequently it figures into the narrative, or provides meaningful commentary in some way. It merits mentioning that the filmmakers who use music in this way tend to be slightly out of the mainstream, although some have achieved mainstream success with certain movies. In the category of films that use pre-existent classical music in this way, we might include Wes Anderson's Benjamin Britten-heavy score for *Moonrise Kingdom* (2012) and the Coen brothers' use of Beethoven in *The Man Who Wasn't There* (2001).

One filmmaker whose use of classical music and newly composed cues seems to echo Kubrick's modus operandi is Terrence Malick. A notoriously reclusive filmmaker, who shares Kubrick's penchant for long pre-production periods, Malick has shown a taste for newly composed tracks alongside pre-existent classical music as we see in Kubrick's scores from *2001* onwards. Malick's scores to *Days of Heaven* (1978), *The New World* (2005), *The Tree of Life* (2011), and *Knight of Cups* (2015) all encompass a Kubrickian sensibility and sensitivity to music.

Malick collaborated with Ennio Morricone for the score to *Days of Heaven*, sharing selections he'd made for a temporary track (*Film Score Monthly* 2011). In this collection of pre-existent works were Morricone's own score for Bernardo Bertolucci's *Novecento* and Camille Saint-Saëns' "Aquarium" from *Carnival of the Animals*. In hearing this music together, Malick and Morricone worked out how new music and pre-existent music would coexist on the score. Asking composers to work around pre-existent music is nothing new, although in many cases it is at the behest of production executives who want to increase energy and marketability in a movie with more popular song choices for the soundtrack album. Having a director meet up with a composer early in production to discuss these kinds of "temp-track" issues is less common, but suggests an attempt at both transparency and communication, something Kubrick found useful after *2001: A Space Odyssey*.

In Malick's *The Tree of Life* music is part of the narrative. The character of Mr. O'Brien states, "Don't do like I did [. . .] I dreamed of being a great musician. I let myself get sidetracked." The music underneath this dialogue is Mr. O'Brien playing Bach's *Toccata* and *Fugue in D minor*. He laments giving up his passion for music in order to work at a power plant, but there are a few scenes of his character sharing music with his sons. Much of Malick's chosen pre-existent music appears on the score alongside Alexandre Desplat's newly written cues. Malick outdid himself with sheer volume and variety—over three dozen pieces, which include selections from Respighi, Smetana, Mahler, Brahms, Górecki, and Couperin. Malick was very forthcoming with Desplat on how he was going to use the new music. Although only a few of Desplat's cues appear in the film, the official soundtrack album contains only his music, including the cues that did not make it into the film.

Because of his transparency in using both pre-existent music and newly composed cues, Malick has found willing collaborators in Morricone, Desplat, and Hanan Townshend, with whom he worked on *To the Wonder* (2012) and who was both performer and music licensee on *The Tree of Life*. But this practice is not without pitfalls. Late composer James Horner found his personal experience with Malick disappointing. In 2005, Horner worked on the score for *The New World*, and his score—like North's for *2001*—was ultimately abandoned. In an interview with Daniel Schweiger for Film Music Radio, Horner said of the experience "I never felt so letdown by a filmmaker in my life" (quoted in Jagernauth 2015). Choosing pre-existent music for a film, and wanting a living and working composer to respect those choices, is not always going to work, although Kubrick and Malick prove that it can be done.

Stanley Kubrick's musical legacy is in many ways defined by *2001: A Space Odyssey*. The subtleties of the musical choices he made in films before and after are often lost in the iconic score of Richard Strauss, Johann Strauss, Jr., and Ligeti. Writing about *2001* and Alex North's score have dominated scholarship about Kubrick's music since the 2000s (Cohen 2000; Merkley 2007; Heimerdinger 2011; McQuiston 2011; Gengaro 2012). To see a more nuanced picture of Kubrick's use of music, and how this use encompassed new compositions, period-appropriate popular songs, arrangements, and recordings of classical music, is to begin to understand how Kubrick affected film scores of the last 50 years, and indeed the way filmmakers and audiences experience music in film. There is perhaps no non-musician so responsible for such a significant shift in scoring methods. In the 1920s and 30s, the move away from pre-existent classical music was an organic evolution; the move towards its use again is part of the legacy of Kubrick and particularly of *2001: A Space Odyssey*. The ideal of Kubrick, as auteur, as the so-called reclusive genius, still resonates with filmmakers learning their craft into the twenty-first century. Considering that some of the most successful directors working today such as Wes Anderson, the Coen brothers, Quentin Tarantino, Martin Scorsese, and Terrence Malick echo Kubrick's methods, there is no doubt that we will continue to see—and hear—Kubrick's influence for years to come.

Works cited

Anon. "2001: A Space Odyssey." *Fandom Wiki*. http://2001.wikia.com/wiki/List_of_references_to_2001:_A_Space_Odyssey.

Agel, Jerome. 1970. *The Making of Kubrick's 2001*. New York: Signet.

Broderick, Mick. 2017. "Post Kubrick: on the Filmmakers Influence and Legacy." *Screening the Past*, no. 42. www.screeningthepast.com/2017/09/post-kubrick-on-the-filmmakers-influence-and-legacy/.

Byrnes, Paul. 2013. "Kubrick Knew the Score, and He Used It." *Sydney Morning Herald*, January 14. www.smh.com.au/entertainment/movies/kubrick-knew-the-score-and-he-used-it-20130114-2cpnb.html.

Ciment, Michel. 1999. *Kubrick: The Definitive Edition*. Translated by Gilbert Adair. New York: Faber and Faber.

Cohen, Richard. 2000. "A Practical Guide to Re-hearing *2001*." *New York Review of Science Fiction* 12, no. 7: 10–14.

Cooke, Mervyn. 2008. *A History of Film Music*. New York: Cambridge University Press.

Darby, William, and Jack DuBois. 1990. *American Film Music: Major Composers, Techniques, Trends 1915–1990*. Jefferson, NC: McFarland.

"Days of Heaven CD Review." 2011. *Film Score Monthly*, July 22. www.filmscoremonthly.com/cds/detail.cfm/CDID/474/Days-of-Heaven/.

Ebert, Roger. 1997. "2001: A Space Odyssey." March 27. www.rogerebert.com/reviews/great-movie-2001-a-space-odyssey-1968.

Gengaro, Christine Lee. 2012. *Listening to Stanley Kubrick: The Music in His Films*. Lanham, MD: Scarecrow Press.

Heimerdinger, Julia. 2011. "'I Have Been Compromised: I Am Now Fighting Against It': Ligeti vs. Kubrick and the Music for *2001: A Space Odyssey*." *Journal of Film Music* 3, no. 2: 127–43.

Henderson, Sanya Shoilevska. 1993. *Alex North, Film Composer*. Jefferson, NC: McFarland.

Hickman, Roger. 2006. *Reel Music: Exploring 100 Years of Film Music*. New York: W.W. Norton and Company.
Jagernauth, Kevin. 2015. "James Horner Says Terrence Malick 'Doesn't Know How to Coalesce a Film from Beginning to End.'" *IndieWire*, May 4. www.indiewire.com/2015/05/james-horner-says-terrence-malick-doesnt-know-how-to-coalesce-a-story-from-beginning-to-end-264433/.
Kolker, Robert P. 2015. "The Imaginary Museum: Martin Scorsese's Film History Documentaries." In *A Companion to Martin Scorsese*, edited by Aaron Baker, 71–90. Chichester: John Wiley and Sons.
Lash, Dominic. 2017. "Distance Listening: Musical Anachronism in Stanley Kubrick's *Barry Lyndon*." *Cinergie-Il cinema e le alter arti*, no. 12: 83–93.
Levinson, Peter J. 2001. *September in the Rain: The Life of Nelson Riddle*. New York: Billboard Books.
LoBrutto, Vincent. 1999. *Stanley Kubrick: A Biography*. New York: Da Capo Press.
Marshall, Colin. 2014. "Quentin Tarantino Explains the Art of Music in His Films." *Open Culture*, September 3. www.openculture.com/2014/09/quentin-tarantino-the-art-of-the-music-in-his-films.html.
McQuiston, Katherine. 2011. "'An Effort to Decide': More Research into Kubrick's Music Choices for *2001: A Space Odyssey*." *Journal of Film Music* 3, no. 2: 145–54.
Merkley, Paul. 2007. "'Stanley Hates This But I Like It!': North vs. Kubrick on the Music for *2001: A Space Odyssey*." *The Journal of Film Music* 2, no. 1: 1–34.
Monahan, Mark. 2002. "Filmmakers on Film: Frank Darabont." *Telegraph*, May 25. www.telegraph.co.uk/culture/film/3578079/Filmmakers-on-film-Frank-Darabont.html.
Music Inspired by MGM's Presentation of the Stanley Kubrick Production 2001: A Space Odyssey. 1968. MGM, MMF 1018.
Rapée, Ernö. (1924) 1974. *Motion Picture Moods for Pianists and Organists*. Reprint, New York: Arno.
Ross, Alex. 2016. "Listening to *Star Wars*." *The New Yorker*, January 1. www.newyorker.com/culture/cultural-comment/listening-to-star-wars.
Schultheis, Bernd. 2007. "Expanse of Possibilities: Stanley Kubrick's Soundtracks in Notes." In *Stanley Kubrick Catalogue*, 2nd ed., 266–79. Frankfurt am Main: Deutsches Filmmuseum.
Swed, Mark. 2010. "Critic's Notebook: 'Shutter Island' as a New-Music Haven." *The Los Angeles Times*, February 24.
Thomas, Tony. 1979. *Film Score: The View from the Podium*. South Brunswick, NJ: A.S. Barnes.

5 Dramatizing Kubrick

Room 237 and other conspiracies

Manca Perko

In his review of *Room 237* (2012), film critic Jim Emerson (2013) dismissed all credibility of the featured, controversial interpretations of Stanley Kubrick's *The Shining* (1980) as the babble of "conspirators—er, contributors" who, under pretense of analysis, impose their extreme readings of hidden meanings, which were, allegedly, intentionally instilled in the film by the director himself. For Emerson (2013, para. 2): "'Room 237' isn't film criticism, it isn't coherent analysis, but listening to fanatics go on and on about their fixations can be kind of fun. For a while, at least." Emerson's blunt criticism served to focus the debate over both the quality and value of film interpretation employed by the audiences of Kubrick's films.

Years after Kubrick's death his films continue to be the subject of discussion and analyses over inter-textual meanings and, as such, reflect the on-going impact of Kubrick's legacy within popular culture. The deliberate ambiguity of his films and Kubrick's reluctance to provide an authoritative reading of his works encourage re-viewing and re-interpretation which at times result in readings at the borderline of folly and farce.

It is now plausible to claim that the value of expertise in evaluating art has been minimized to the point of popular culture disregarding professional assessment and quality of the critique. Hence, I examine the processes in relation to this phenomenon by studying some of the more extreme readings of Kubrick's *The Shining* (1980) presented in Rodney Ascher's documentary *Room 237* (2012) and other 'conspiracy' theories, circulating in popular culture, such as YouTube videos of Kubrick's alleged confession to filming the moon landing, and in-depth explanations of it as seen in *Dark Side of the Moon: Stanley Kubrick and the Fake Moon Landings* (Dir: William Karel 2002/2014).

This study addresses such borderline readings with the intention to demonstrate how representation and evaluation of art in popular culture can affect readings of Kubrick's films and the perception of his legacy in social and cultural context. My analysis of the 'spurious' readings of Kubrick's works will reference the scholarship of I. Q. Hunter (2016), Marco Lovisato (2017), David Bordwell (2013), Catriona McAvoy (2015), Laura Mee (2017) and the philosophical approaches to studying art via Immanuel Kant's critique of judgment (in Burnham 2018), the philosophical evaluation of expertise, and Umberto Eco's (1990) observations on the overinterpretation of texts as a modern engagement theory of the relativity of meaning. I juxtapose evaluations of meaning crafted by both 'experts' and 'amateurs' in an attempt to define their competency in passing judgment on the readings, what criteria are used and how that affects both the works of art in question and their creators. My argument is that representation and evaluation of art in popular culture affects readings of Kubrick's films and the perception of his legacy in social and cultural contexts.

Interpretation of Kubrick's films long ago left the domain of theorists and film critics. By ease of access to his work through video and DVD release, and increasingly via communication over the internet, multiple interpretations extend further into popular culture. Lovisato refers to the modern recipients of films as "the film consumers of the internet era" who form a new cinematographic spectatorship practice—modern cinephilia (2017, 128–29). Global consumerism has aided the formation of online social groups who practice evaluation of creative products with or without founding their criticism within theoretical tradition or professional knowledge of film production.[1] While this practice promotes the "audience's self-reflexivity," it also decreases the value of critical readings (Hunter 2016, 47). Mee observes: "In the digital age, everyone is a critic, and credentials are not essential for film analysis" (2017, 155). Albeit the amateur interpreters are free to do so, the quality of feedback is questionable.

As creators of meanings, filmmakers often have their own reading of the produced text disregarded, misinterpreted, and even manipulated by the audience. Some filmmakers began to defy this limiting phenomenon of devaluating of their art by employing techniques to avoid oversimplification. Kubrick tended to avoid this by deliberately instilling ambiguity of meaning in his films. As Hunter (2016, 47) points out, Kubrick's films intentionally encourage the audience to interpret them "holistically and conspiratorially." Kubrick often challenged entrenched critical interpretations and publicly encouraged the audience to discover the meaning for themselves, as he explained:

> Some people demand a five-line capsule summary. Something you'd read in a magazine. They want you to say, "This is the story of the duality of man and the duplicity of governments." I hear people try to do it—give the five-line summary—but if a film has any substance or subtlety, whatever you say is never complete, it's usually wrong, and

it's necessarily simplistic: truth is too multifaceted to be contained in a five-line summary. If the work is good, what you say about it is usually irrelevant.

(Cahill 2011)

The predominant issue with interpretation of meaning lies in the complexity of the process, which Eco (1990, 183) depicts as a "sophisticated strategy of interplay between the readers of the texts and their competence in language as a social treasury." The interaction between the interpreting subject and the process they employ generates the understanding of meaning and the intention of the creative producer. Before addressing the specifics of this interplay, it is necessary to understand what the "language" used in the process of reading actually is.

According to numerous theorists (e.g. Metz 1991) over time, the language employed by a reader of a text is a puzzle of codes of representation (Hall 1997). These codes function as symbols and are involved in the creation of meaning. At the same time, they form a language of interpretation which the audience (professional, academic, or general film viewers) employ in their readings of meaning (Metz 1991; Culler 1988). Hence, in my later analysis of *Room 237* and in process of evaluating screen art I will demonstrate specific cinematic codes and the role of interpretation. However, at this point I will focus on the communication between the 'creator' and the reader of the text, addressing the exchange of cinematic codes.

Umberto Eco posits that the meaning of a text is communicated by the language of interpretation, which can be classified as a cluster of "cultural conventions" that have been accumulated from interpretations employed in the past (1990, 183). To clarify Eco's position, cultural conventions can be seen as an array of signs that the audience/reader uses in deciphering the meaning that is encoded in cinematic language, something filmmakers manipulate. In order to exploit the language to encode specific meaning, a filmmaker has to exhibit fluency in it. Kubrick is a prime example of a filmmaker who skillfully manipulated cinematic language, a talent that can be attributed to his eloquence in, and mastery of, the technical features of cinematic language. For example, Kubrick's self-taught expertise in cinematography initially stemmed from his professional background in photography while still a teenager. Kubrick was well aware of the interpretative power of cinematic language, as evident from numerous interviews conducted over decades (Southern 1962; Cahill 1987).

Understanding the cinematic language and the process of its application to achieve a desired effect (e.g. ambiguity of meaning in Kubrick's case) is not a matter of the acuity of the audience, but a matter of the relevance and suitability of interpretation. Competency in the language of interpretation

Dramatizing Kubrick 55

informs Eco's concept (1990) of an accrued "social treasury"—a prerogative based on scholarly expertise in textual analysis and film theory, as well as proficiency in understanding film production practice. Thus, I argue, to find specific meaning in Kubrick's films, the codes have to be identified and validated by knowledge obtained from scholarly precedent and practitioner experience. An analysis based on such evaluation criteria provides a repertoire of signs and their symbolism. In the following case study a variety of conflicting interpretations of Kubrick's films, as presented in Rodney Ascher's documentary *Room 237*, gestures to the lasting impact of Kubrick's legacy.

Room 237 presents readings of *The Shining* by five individuals, different in gender, age, and profession: ABC News journalist Bill Blakemore; Geoffrey Cocks, a historian, specializing in World War II Germany; John Fell Ryan, a film archivist and blogger of textual analyses of Kubrick's films; Jay Weidner, a director and producer of films on Kubrick's work, such as *Kubrick's Odyssey: Secrets Hidden in the Films of Stanley Kubrick; Part One: Kubrick and Apollo* (2011); and playwright Juli Kearns. Ascher's choice of interviewees also broadly represents a general film audience—academics/critics and other film experts, film industry workers (practitioners), and individuals with other professional and non-professional profiles. Opting for a versatile representation pattern, Ascher encompasses the audience from a socio-cultural point of view.

The origin of knowledge employed in interpreting Kubrick's films affects the validity of their readings. My argument is that the newfound social accessibility of information and the corresponding freedom to publicly deploy criticism should not overshadow the prerequisite knowledge in the field of Kubrick's cinema. For example, when interpreting miscellaneous phenomena, philosophers often employ the concept of ontology. Although these approaches are in essence highly theoretical, they can be applied to reading film. Basing his work on film's aesthetics philosopher Berys Gaut (2007) links the ontology of interpretation to evaluation of art, aesthetics, and creativity (2010), combining the processes of creation, representation, and evaluation. To illustrate this interconnection, I summarize traditional philosophical approaches to the interpretation of art and extend their historical methodology to interpreting cinema.

The discipline of evaluating art can be traced back to Ancient Greece via Aristotle and Plato in the third and fourth centuries BCE. Plato characterized audience readings as an "imitation of the original nature of true art" (Plato and Shorey 1930). In the "allegory of the cave" Plato defined the mimetic technique of creating and perceiving art, where people could observe an object by its shadow on the wall. Hence their interpretation of the original is only via a copy, a mimesis of its "beauty" (Plato in Shorey 1930).

Plato's metaphor refers to objectivity in evaluation; the audience readings are subjective and can only approach the 'real' interpretation of the original as intended by its creator. However, the Platonic evaluation of meaning was too limiting in determining the legitimacy of interpretations. Aristotle's evaluation criteria were much more applicable as they recognized the need for a 'synthesis' of knowledge (*episteme*) and empirical experience (*technê*), understood today as theory and practice (Aristotle and Rackham 2015). Kant concurred with this application. For a reflective judgment to happen, i.e. to succumb to the 'right' evaluative criteria, Kant maintained certain knowledge has to be present a priori (Burnham 2018). Simultaneously, decoding signs without connecting them to experience diminishes aesthetic engagement because "some components of our beliefs must be brought by the mind to experience" (McCormick 2001).

Therefore, I advocate combining these standard philosophical approaches to the evaluation of the aesthetics of art with contemporary constructivist definitions of cinematic interpretation from the properties of aesthetics: consideration of the use of color, shape, composition, texture, institutional and historical characteristic of an artistic product. Bordwell and Thompson (2010) expand the listed formalist criteria in their neo-formalist approach to evaluating films. They add more specific criteria for evaluating films by analyzing their technical elements, such as lighting, sound, set design, use shot composition, and editing. They frame their arguments in the theoretical traditions of structuralism[2] and post-structuralism,[3] analyzing the interrelations between these non-textual, aesthetic codes as the most valuable criteria in interpreting an artwork (2010, 58).

Referring back to Aristotle and Kant's emphasis on empirical experience, the approach by Bordwell and Thompson appears valid primarily because of its observation and application of technical knowledge manifest in screen production. Similarly, I argue for a 'synthesis' of theory and practice in evaluating films precisely because of the existing discrepancy between the two. In general, critics conventionally base their interpretations on historical or theoretical knowledge whereas film workers draw from practical experience. However, lay audiences can elicit meaning from both approaches to their reading or none of the above. What these perspectives frequently have in common is that they maintain their own analysis to be the 'real' interpretation of meaning. The simple fact that many viewers might not have either practical or theoretical knowledge when reading a text leads to questions over the quality and veracity of their interpretations.

The practice of artistic evaluation has become increasingly associated with the personal opinions any such viewer has of a film, evident in popular culture expressions through social media, such as YouTube videos allegedly featuring Kubrick confessing to filming the moon landing (2015). The

Dramatizing Kubrick 57

problem with this media fakery is multi-faced: not only does it falsely represent Kubrick's legacy, if left unchallenged it also negatively affects the way popular culture perceives Kubrick as an artist. As time goes by more and more of Kubrick's works are misinterpreted, manipulated, and become the fodder of online conspiracy theories, which I address later in the analysis. At same time, from such unqualified misinformation another effect emerges. Reading of texts to generate meaning/interpretation is being devalued as a skill; what was once a discipline and demanded some prerequisite knowledge in the field is now equated with personal opinion. The danger of assuming there is no difference between the two approaches leads to the over-interpretation/misinterpretation of the texts. Eco has noted: "As soon as a text becomes 'sacred' for a certain culture, it becomes subject to the process of suspicious reading and therefore to what is undoubtedly an excess of interpretation" (1990, 169). So, how can we avoid and/or resolve this 'excess'?

In the late nineteenth century Friedrich Nietzsche boldly claimed: "There are only facts—I would say no, facts are just what there aren't, there are only interpretations" (Bittner et al. 2003, 139). Not only does such an assertion dismiss the importance of, say, neo-formalist readings (e.g. Bordwell and Thompson) but it also implies that *all* interpretations are equally valid since their credibility cannot be compared against formal criteria with there being no 'facts.' However, earlier philosophers such as Kant had eschewed the tendency towards extreme relativism by stressing the pragmatic and speculative nature of interpretation: "All interest is ultimately practical and even that of speculative reason is only conditional and is complete in practical use alone" (quoted in Smith 2003, 441–43). Yet, I argue, identifying interpretations as speculations opens up a Pandora's Box of guesses, conjecture, and fabrication.

One possible way to avoid the excesses of analysis is to consider Eco's 'rightness' of interpretation (1990, 169). Eco offers a solution in differentiating between 'sane' and 'paranoiac' interpretations by describing the readers of extreme meaning: "The paranoiac is the person who begins to wonder about [. . .] mysterious motives" (Eco 1990, 166). This phenomenon can be readily observed in *Room 237*. The numerous explanations, observations, assumptions, and speculations about the meaning of *The Shining* have become "wackier and more paranoid" (Smith 2013). Eco's attempt in separating the paranoiac from a 'sane' person (1990, 169) is a good starting point but he neither offers a definition of 'saneness' nor how to identify it (1990, 169). His search for the "rightness of the interpretation" is achieved by first identifying the 'wrong' interpretation in order to promote the 'right' one. I propose another option. The extreme readings, misinterpretations, and over-interpretations can only be identified as such if they are subjected to rational evaluative criteria, whether internal or external.

Internal criteria can originate from two sources. The first is the audience's 'internal' evaluation by which I mean the evaluation based on their perception of features of the creative product—e.g. expressiveness, wholeness (Treffinger, Selby, and Schoonover 2012). This is a fully subjective measurement, equivalent to the method of aesthetic evaluation. The second source of the internal criteria is applicable only to a certain extent in my analysis. It originates from the artist-creator—what is suggested by 'the director meant to say'—i.e. his intention, his 'drive.' Patrick Maynard (2003) explores this option via "intentionalism." Contrary to the previously described formalist view on evaluation that stresses the importance of the correct interpretation of the artwork as the most valuable criteria, intentionalism divines the creative person's intention as that which determines correct interpretations (Gaut and Livingston 2003, 7). But a paradox seems inherent. Intentionalism, the internal source, can be identified by using an external source of evaluation: the audience's internal (subjective) or the audience's external (objective) perception of the creative person's intention. Hence, in order to determine the person's intention one should avoid 'guessing' the intention but be informed of it from the original source—the creators themselves. However, this is not always possible. Some artist-creators do not wish to offer this information, some simply state that they do not have an intention and some are controlled by studios and with little or no input. It follows then that an expressed intention is not a strong enough criterion for evaluating creativity, nor the value of the creative product. It serves merely as an additional tool in understanding the process of transforming the ideas into a product, but in reality, does not affect the validity of interpretation.

At this point both film practitioners and theorists would no doubt protest. Practitioners would claim the intention is the crucible of artistic creation and the theorist-historians likely foreground intentionalism within their interpretations. The difference is that practitioners see intention from two perspectives. First, there could have been an intention in the dramaturgy that affected the filmmaking techniques or, second, it could have been the opposite—no dramatic intentions but simply achieving an aesthetic effect. Theorists, however, do not seem to take this option into account and believe every stylistic technique is deployed with a dramaturgical intention.

In *Room 237* the interpretations of *The Shining* become more complex with socio-historical and cultural contexts for their readings. For example, Geoffrey Cocks introduces a 'Holocaust reading' by noticing a reoccurrence of the number "42," as the year in which the Holocaust had taken the largest number of victims. He claims that Kubrick made an intentional choice with the typewriter branded Adler—in German meaning 'eagle,' which was the symbol of the Nazi-party—and several other prop choices indicating Kubrick's intentional inclusion of Holocaust symbolism. Cocks describes the typewriter as "a German machine, pictured almost to make it a character, a clear representation of the bureaucratic killing machine" (Tracy 2012, para.3). But such theories do not stack up to scrutiny. Kubrick's archive features voluminous research files from *The Shining*'s art department, including photographs and photocopies of typewriters, varying in color, size, and brand. The research was extensive and Cocks' interpretation of Kubrick's prop choice as intentional coding of the SS symbol, does not withstand examination via the historical repository or from in situ collaborators. As Kubrick's assistant, Leon Vitali, has confirmed: "That was Stanley's typewriter. A lot of decisions made on the set were about pragmatism: 'This looks good. It sits on the oak table pretty perfectly.' Not to mention, it's a great typewriter. I used that typewriter for 10 years, actually" (Segal 2013).

The Holocaust theme is open to many legitimate interpretations within Kubrick's films. Nathan Abrams, author of *Stanley Kubrick: New York Jewish Intellectual* (2018), alongside other academics, such as Cocks, author of *The Wolf at the Door: Stanley Kubrick, History, and the Holocaust* (2005), have detailed instances of this theme within the Kubrick Archive and from interviews with his collaborators. It is now well documented that Kubrick's development and pre-production of his Holocaust film, *Aryan Papers*, was abandoned partly due to the release of Spielberg's *Schindler's List* (1993). While Kubrick was well advanced in creating such a film, to presume that he purposely set clues for its future manifestation in his earlier films is exactly that—only a presumption. Developing his idea further in *Room 237*, Cocks discusses a dissolving transition shot of people in the Overlook Hotel lobby over the accompanying shot of the Torrance family's suitcases. He decodes this as referencing the transportation of Jews into concentration camps, leaving their suitcases behind. I acknowledge Cocks' respectful record of academic research, however in *Room 237* his interpretation is no longer speculation. It is, in P.D. Smith (2013), Lovisato (2017), and Eco's (1990) words, a 'wacky' reading of a text. *In Room 237*, Cocks joins the collective of subjects who "blur the line between rational and paranoid interpretation" (Hunter 2016, 47).

Similarly, in *Room 237*, Blakemore insists that *The Shining* is about American Indians. The documentary begins with his interpretation of *The Shining*'s marketing slogan "The tide of terror that swept America is HERE" which Blakemore describes as a metaphor of the "white man's invasion and annihilation of the Indians." He further decodes this theme from props used by the art department—"broken dishonest pipe treaties" symbolized by cans of Calumet baking powder displayed in the Overlook's storage room—and finally poses a rhetorical question: "How come I saw this and a lot of other people didn't?" The reactions from Kubrick's practitioner-collaborators to such claims are not surprising. Vitali rejects most of the interpretations in *Room 237*. He was exasperated, for example, by Kearns' interpretation of the poster of a downhill skier on the wall of the Overlook's game room. Kearns believes it to be a Minotaur, intentionally placed there to associate Jack Torrance with the half-bull-half-human creature from Greek mythology and to remind the audience of the maze-like structure of the film. However, Vitali noted: "I stood staring at all that stuff for weeks while we were shooting in that room. It's a downhill skier. It's a downhill skier. It's not a Minotaur" (Segal 2013).

Why such readings become so radical over time might be explained with Fell Ryan's observation: "When you see things over and over things change for you" (2012). Camera movement, acting, and especially the assumed symbolism of props—everything seems to have a connection. The extremes to which these readings go is rather astonishing, such as the suggestion of subliminal sexual signs intentionally included in the film (the hotel manager's symbolic "hard-on" when greeting Jack), or by interpreting Jack Torrance's sinisterly comic line "little pigs, little pigs, let me in" as referencing anti-Semitism. Vitali dismisses outright the idea of Kubrick intentionally using a reference to this children's story in order to insert clues of the Holocaust in *The Shining*, attributing the line solely to Jack Nicholson's improvisation on the set (Segal 2013).

Towards the end of *Room 237*, the over-interpretations spiral. The conspiracy theories concerning Kubrick's so-called 'faked' moon landing footage, "kept secret by NASA" (but recently 'leaked' to YouTube and 'revealed' in the *Dark Side of The Moon*), originate from audiences reading alleged covert 'signs' in the film, such as the Apollo rocket sweater worn by Danny Torrance. These readings are not supported by any factual, documented evidence concerning the filmmaker's creative intentions, nor from a synthesis of theoretical and practical knowledge of cinematic codes. They are merely assumptions and interpretations constituting individual opinions based on a reader 'decoding' the use of one instance of character attire. As Lovisato says: "Here cinemania truly seems to lose touch with reality, and searching for truth no longer matters" (2017, 133). To exemplify another extreme misreading presented in *Room 237*, one that emanates from an individual's imagination, devoid of praxis or theory based on the text, one interviewee claims that Kubrick's face is deliberately morphed into the clouds above the mountains in the title sequence and visible on approach to the Overlook Hotel. This absurdity is further exceeded with Fell Ryan screening *The Shining* backwards and forwards simultaneously while textually analyzing the images that overlap. Such practice is typical for the consumer as a "producer of new contents" who constructs new audio-visual material by remixing the existent source (Lovisato 2017, 128–29).

The primary problem here lies in the extent to which the readers go to justify their speculations, a process Lovisato refers to as "cinemania" (2017, 133). They are reluctant to have an open mind to various interpretations and the actual interpretation of the creative work becomes increasingly that of a dogmatic reading. Whereas Nietzsche may have denied the certainty and veracity of 'facts,' he nevertheless stressed that "However strongly something is believed, that is not a criterion of truth" (Bittner et al. 2003, 43). It is often difficult to treat any of this interpretation seriously, as critic Matt Goldberg (2012) humorously reflected in regard to *Room 237*:

> It's hilarious when one critic begins an attempt to prove that *The Shining* is Kubrick's secret confession about filming the fake moon landing. The critic prefaces his theory by saying, "I'm not saying that we didn't go to the moon. I'm just saying that the footage was faked." And then he starts pointing out Danny's Apollo 11 shirt, the fact that the moon is roughly 237,000 miles from Earth, and (my personal favourite) he notes that the 237 room key reads 'Room No. 237.' There's only two words you can spell, notes the critic, "'Room'... and 'moon'." After the screening, I overheard someone say, "You can also spell 'moron'."

Clearly some audience members genuinely believe that they see 'clues' encoded in the text and some experts among them strive to support their readings theoretically and praxiologically. McAvoy (2015) believes this happens because the audiences are on a quest for "mystical meanings" to help them solve the mysteries. However, these readings remain too fixed. If one criterion for evaluating the creative product is its ability to be subjected to re-reading why do the audience interpretations rarely change over the course of time? Kubrick pondered the same:

> People can misinterpret almost anything so that it coincides with views they already hold. They take from art what they already believe, and I wonder how many people have ever had their views about anything important changed by a work of art?
>
> (Ciment 1984, 196)

The phenomenon can be usefully examined from a social perspective. In order to operate within the creative industries, film practitioners comply with the 'habitus' (Bordieau 1986) of the industry's environment. For example, a commercial producer often implements certain ethical restrictions (e.g. the U.K. Video Recordings Act's tests of suitability potential for under-age viewing) or legislative restrictions mandated on the industry (e.g. British Board of Film Classifications 2018). The same habitus applies to the consumers of art and commerce; they interact in evaluating a product by applying a consensus criteria set by the social framework: "The audience, for its part, will receive the film according to the readerly codes of film consumption and the film's relation to the contemporary social context" (Saxton 1986, 22). The process of social (inter)action brings focus back to a common external evaluative criteria—the audience's perception of the author's intention. Such practice corresponds to Eco's differentiation between the "empirical" and "model" author (1990, 187–88). The readers take one or the other into account; Kubrick as the model author, "which is nothing else than an explicit textual strategy" and Kubrick as the empirical author, questioning his intention. Kubrick persistently avoided clarifying his intention, as observed in his answer when challenged about inserting a 'secret code' in *Full Metal Jacket* (Cahill 2011):

> When Cowboy is shot, they carry him around the corner—to the very most logical shelter. And there, in the background, was this thing, this monolith. I'm sure some people will think that there was some calculated reference to *2001*, but honestly, it was just there.

Cahill insisted: "You don't think you're going to get away with that, do you?" and Kubrick laughed: "I know it's an amazing coincidence" (2011).

Kubrick's reluctance to share his artistic intentions might be, as he noted himself in this particular instance, because there was no intention. His response corresponds to Eco's observation of a discrepancy between the author's production and reader's reception of the text: "The author knows that he or she will be interpreted not according to his or her intentions but according to a complex strategy of interactions which also involve the readers, along with their competence in language as a social treasury" (1990, 187–88). This suggests that Kubrick deliberately embraced a reluctance to articulate authorial intentionality and not limit an audience's readings. His lack of authorial clarification opens an array of possible interpretations for the viewers, resulting in contradictory and potentially extreme outcomes.

Generations of semioticians and cultural critics have demonstrated that audiences/readers, as the receivers of the texts, are also the creators of meaning.[4] They actively engage in interpreting cultural production that is implicitly ambiguous in its meaning, allowing each individual to form their own ideas. This coincides with Barthes' (Barthes and Heath 1977) concept of 'death of the author': whichever idea, image, or action the consumers employ, it already exists and is only a mixture of cultural and social experiences, combined with past knowledge. Here lies the problem. Various individual interpretations can be seen as "tissues of quotations" (Barthes and Heath 1977) formed from the existing cultural archive. Not only do the interpretations defy their originality, they result in an (over)abundance of interpretations, which in effect can lead to misinterpretations and overinterpretations of texts, questioning the validity of interpretations and the value of evaluation process.

Openness to interpretation is a predominant feature of Kubrick's films. In the 1960s Kubrick repeatedly rejected the idea that film viewing should be a one-off activity, equating cinema with modes of music where one returns to a work over and over again for pleasure and edification. Ambiguity, re-reading, and re-interpreting for future generations perpetuates his artistic stature and legacy. Kubrick actively endorsed this feature by promoting his works as intrinsically enigmatic. Cahill asked him: "Well, you don't make it easy on viewers or critics. [. . .] You create strong feelings, but you won't give us any easy answers," to which Kubrick responded: "That's because I don't have any easy answers" (Cahill 2011).

Ambiguity of meaning was Kubrick's 'choice of weapon' in assuring his works would be discussed for years to come. The quality of audience readings, however, remains problematic. If we consider Kubrick's films as works of art, which we increasingly and demonstrably do, then readings not based on criteria for evaluating art may inevitably result in devaluing such cultural production. An implication is that Kubrick's films will be diminished as will his reputation as a major twentieth-century artist.

My analysis of the readings of Kubrick's *The Shining*, presented in the documentary *Room 237*, was inspired by the contemporary flood of over-interpretations and misinterpretations of Kubrick's oeuvre. This phenomenon is problematic in two ways. First, the diminishing effect it has on technical expertise and the validity of orthodox interpretations and, second, its impact on the portrayal of Kubrick's legacy in popular culture. I approached the individual readings in *Room 237* from a social and cultural perspective, considering the process of interpretation and interaction between the readers of the texts and the language employed in the process which Bordwell (2013) defines as "free play of the signifier." To present fully applicable criteria for the interpretation of Kubrick's work and to surpass the audience's practice of applying their "own cinematic religiosity" to the readings of his films (McAvoy 2015), I included historical and philosophical approaches in assessing creative works. I separated interpretation from speculation and differentiated knowledge that is based on theory (employed by film academics, critics, and reviewers) from knowledge obtained through praxis (film practitioners) which suggested a need for a *synthesis* that would provide more comprehensive criteria for evaluating Kubrick's films.

Kubrick consciously preserved the ambiguity of meaning in his deeply researched and multi-layered films that has ensured re-interpretation of his work from audiences repeatedly viewing his films: "Kubrick's *The Shining* is particularly suitable for repeated compulsive viewing that encourages sensory overload and a potentially infinite cycle of interpretations" (Lovisato 2017, 127). The strategy succeeded. The ease of access to his oeuvre via home video, then DVD, special editions, streaming services, and internet sites (videos, documentaries, interviews, etc.) has expanded his legacy into the twenty-first century. While virtually anyone today can engage with his work and give their opinion, a practice which Hunter (2016) and Mee (2017) recognize as dangerous to critical readings, the validity of these individual interpretations affects the value of Kubrick's cinema as works of art. It challenges expertise in hermeneutics and critique as a skill and, consequently, erodes traditions of professional knowledge. As a result, such 'unprofessional' evaluation of his oeuvre may devalue the understanding of Kubrick's films as works of art. One possible way to curtail the overreach of interpretation is the *synthesis* of *episteme* and *technê* on the assessment of Kubrick's legacy to introduce new insights by comparing the normative restrictions of film industry *habitus*, then and now. Perhaps Kubrick's legacy could be best assessed by joining *theory* and *practice* into *phronesis* (practical wisdom or mindfulness).

Notes

1 See The Kubrick Site (2018).
2 Claude Lévi-Strauss, 1908–2009 (Craig 1998).
3 Jacques Derrida, 1930–2004 (Craig 1998).
4 *Saussure* (Culler 1988).

Works cited

Abrams, Nathan. 2012. *The New Jew in Film Exploring Jewishness and Judaism in Contemporary Cinema*. London: I.B. Tauris.
Aristotle, and Harris, Rackham. 2015. *Nicomachean Ethics*. Cambridge, MA: Harvard University Press.
Ascher, Rodney. 2012. *Room 237*. Film. USA: Highland Park Classics.
Barthes, Roland, and Heath, Stephen. 1977. *Image, Music, Text*. London: Fontana Press.
Bittner, Rüdiger, Friedrich Wilhelm Nietzsche, and Kate Sturge. 2003. *Writings from the late notebooks*. Cambridge, UK: Cambridge University Press.
Bordwell, David. 2013. "All Play and No Work? ROOM 237." *David Bordwell's Website on Cinema*. www.davidbordwell.net/blog/2013/04/07/all-play-and-no-work-room-237/.

Dramatizing Kubrick 65

Bordwell, David, and Kristin, Thompson. 2010. *Film Art: An Introduction*. 3rd ed. New York: McGraw-Hill.

Bourdieu, Pierre. 1986. "The forms of capital." In *Handbook of Theory and Research for the Sociology of Education*, edited by John G. Richardson, 241–258. Westport, CT: Greenwood Press. www.socialcapitalgateway.org/sites/socialcapitalgateway.org/files/data/paper/2016/10/18/rbasicsbourdieu1986-theformsofcapital.pdf.

Burnham, Douglas. 2018. "Kant, Immanuel: Aesthetics | Internet Encyclopedia of Philosophy." *Iep.utm.edu*. www.iep.utm.edu/kantaest/#SH2d.

Cahill, Tim. 2011. "The Rolling Stone Interview: Stanley Kubrick in 1987." *Rolling Stone*. www.rollingstone.com/culture/news/the-rolling-stone-interview-stanley-kubrick-in-1987-20110307.

Ciment, Michel. 1984. *Kubrick*. New York: Holt, Rinehart, and Winston.

"Claimed Stanley Kubrick Confession to Faking the Moon Landings." *YouTube*. 2015. www.youtube.com/watch?v=rfKL27MgaQo.

Cocks, Geoffrey. 2004. *The Wolf at the Door: Stanley Kubrick, History, and the Holocaust*. New York: Peter Lang Publishing, Inc.

Craig, Edward. 1998. *Routledge Encyclopedia of Philosophy, Vol. 7: Nihilism—Quantum Mechanics*. London: Routledge.

Culler, Jonathan D. 1988. *Saussure*. London: Fontana.

Dingus, Duke. 2014. "Dark Side of the Moon—Stanley Kubrick and the Fake Moon Landings." *YouTube*. www.youtube.com/watch?v=4toI9Ujv-pw.

Eco, Umberto. 1990. "Interpretation and Overinterpretation: World, History, Texts." In *The Tanner Lectures on Human Values*, 143–202. Cambridge: Clare Hall, Cambridge University.

Emerson, Jim. 2013. "Room 237 Movie Review and Film Summary (2013) | Roger Ebert." *Rogerebert.com*. www.rogerebert.com/reviews/room-237-2013.

Fell Ryan, John. *Room 237*. Film. Directed by Rodney Ascher. 2012. USA: Highland Park Classics.

Gaut, Berys Nigel. 2010. "The Philosophy of Creativity." *Philosophy Compass* 5, no. 12: 1034–1046. https://onlinelibrary.wiley.com/doi/abs/10.1111/j.1747-9991.2010.00351.x.

Gaut, Berys Nigel. 2007. *Art, Emotion and Ethics*. Oxford: Oxford University Press.

Gaut, Berys Nigel, and Paisley, Livingston. 2003. *The Creation of Art*. Cambridge, UK: Cambridge University Press.

Goldberg, Matt. 2012. "Sundance 2012: ROOM 237 Review." *Collider*. www.collider.com/room-237-review.

Hall, Stuart. 1997. *Representation: Cultural Representations and Signifying Practices*. London: Sage Publications Ltd.

Hunter, I. Q. 2016. *Cult Film as a Guide to Life: Fandom, Adaptation and Identity*. New York: Bloomsbury.

Kubrick, Stanley. 1980. *The Shining*. Film. UK, USA: Warner Bros., Hawk Films, Peregrine Producers Circle.

———. 1987. *Full Metal Jacket*. Film. UK: Natant, Stanley Kubrick Productions, Warner Bros.

"The Kubrick Site." 2018. *Visual-memory.co.uk*. www.visual-memory.co.uk/amk/.

"Legislation: Film Licensing." 2018. *British Board of Film Classifications*. www.bbfc.co.uk/education-resources/student-guide/legislation.

Lovisato, Marco. 2017. "(Do Not) Overlook: Room 237 and the Dismemberment of the Shining." *Cinergie Il Cinema e le altre*, Arti 12. doi:10.6092/issn.2280-9481/7351.

Maynard, Patrick. 2003. "Drawings as Drawn: An Approach to Creation in an Art." In *The Creation of Art: New Essays in Philosophical Aesthetics*, edited by Berys Gaut and Paisley Livingston, 53–88. Cambridge: Cambridge University Press.

McAvoy, Catriona. 2015. "The Uncanny, The Gothic and The Loner: Intertextuality in the Adaptation Process of The Shining." *Adaptation* 8, no. 3: 345–60. https://doi.org/10.1093/adaptation/apv012.

McCormick, Matt. 2001. "Kant, Immanuel: Metaphysics." *Internet Encyclopedia of Philosophy*. www.iep.utm.edu/kantmeta/.

Mee, Laura. 2017. "Room 237: Cinephilia, History and Adaptation." In *The Past in Visual Culture: Essays on Memory, Nostalgia and the Media*, edited by Jilly Boyce Kay et al., 154–67. Jefferson, NC: McFarland & Company.

Metz, Christian. 1991. *Film Language*. Chicago: University of Chicago Press.

Plato, and Paul, Shorey. 1930. *The Republic*. London: W. Heinemann.

Prop and Set Dressing Research and Development, 1987, SK/15/2/2. Stanley Kubrick Archive. University of the Arts London.

Saxton, Christine. 1986. "The Collective Voice as Cultural Voice." *Cinema Journal* 26, no. 1: 19–30. JSTOR. doi:10.2307/1224984.

Segal, David. 2013. "Aide to Kubrick on 'Shining' Scoffs at 'Room 237' Theories." *Nytimes.com*. www.nytimes.com/2013/03/31/movies/aide-to-kubrick-on-shining-scoffs-at-room-237-theories.html.

Smith, Norman Kemp. 2003. *A Commentary to Kant's 'Critique of Pure Reason'*. Houndmills, Basingstoke, Hampshire: Palgrave Macmillan.

Smith, P. D. 2013. "The Shining by Roger Luckhurst—Review." *The Guardian*. www.theguardian.com/books/2013/nov/15/shining-roger-luckhurst-review.

Southern, Terry. 1962. "An Interview with Stanley Kubrick, Director of Lolita." Unpublished. The Terry Southern Estate. www.archiviokubrick.it/english/words/interviews/1962southern.html.

Tracy, Marc. 2012. "What Makes Stanley Kubrick's 'The Shining' a Holocaust Film." *Tablet Magazine*. www.tabletmag.com/scroll/89719/kubrick%E2%80%99s-holocaust-film.

Treffinger, Donald J., Edwin C. Selby, and Patricia Schoonover. 2012. "Creativity in the Person: Contemporary Perspectives." *Creativity: Insights, Directions and Possibilities* 6, no. 1: 409–19. www.learninglandscapes.ca/.

Weidner, Jay. 2011. *Kubrick's Odyssey: Secrets Hidden in the Films of Stanley Kubrick; Part One: Kubrick and Apollo*. DVD. USA: Cubed Brick Productions.

West, Kevin. 2009. "Foucault's Pendulum and the Hermeneutics of Umberto Eco." *Faithandtheacademy.files.wordpress.com*. https://faithandtheacademy.files.wordpress.com/2011/11/2009-02-west.pdf.

6 Kubrick

Tropes in advertising

James Marinaccio

Some of the "most spectacular examples of film art are in the best TV commercials," said film director Stanley Kubrick in a 1987 interview for *Rolling Stone Magazine* with Tim Cahill. Asked for an example Kubrick continued,

> The Michelob commercials. I'm a pro-football fan, and I have videotapes of the games sent over to me, commercials and all. Last year Michelob did a series, just impressions of people having a good time [. . .] the editing, the photography, was some of the most brilliant work I've ever seen. Forget what they're doing—selling beer—and it's visual poetry.
>
> (Cahill 1987)

Television advertisements have been broadcast in the United States from as far back as 1941 (Openculture.com 2013). Print advertising, naturally, goes back considerably further. These, as well as other forms of media, use a familiar array of tactics to grab the consumer's attention and attempt maximum impact in order to sell their product (Croteau and Hoynes 2000). Some common tactics employed by advertising agencies repeatedly include humor, jingles, and the use of a character created specifically for that campaign (Olenski 2012). A frequently adopted tactic is associating your product with someone or something well-known. This deliberate or inferred product association often involves the use of a celebrity or using a piece of well-known popular music (Stockfelt 2010). While perhaps a less common tactic, advertisers have been known to use consumer awareness of iconic movies to catch their attention.

For the purpose of this essay, however, I will not address strategies or tactics employed by film studios or individual filmmakers to market their own films. That is an entirely different exercise.[1] Here I am specifically discussing the selling of products using film iconography; be it cars or soap or coffee or whatever else. So, whether it is Anthony Perkins playing Norman

Bates in a 1990 advertisement for Oatmeal Crisp (wtcvidman 2011) or a young girl suddenly channeling her inner Don Corleone during a Pepsi ad from the 1980s (mjs269 2011) the reference to film is unmistakable. However, the movie association may be far more subtle. It can be as slight as a single line of dialogue, or an image, or a snippet of music, or some other identifiable detail from the film.

This observation led me to question which film or which film director has been referenced the most in advertising? Answering that question is almost impossible to quantify. But as a long-time collector of Stanley Kubrick memorabilia I have been personally alert in noticing when his films are referenced in such ways. So much so that in the mid-1980s I began videotaping all that I saw. From my own broad observations over decades I can say, although not empirically, that it seems Stanley Kubrick's films appear more than any other movie-maker for marketing references; in fact *any* type of reference.

Writing for *Off-Screen* Magazine, David Church provided further insight into why Kubrick may appeal to those both attempting to be artistic and sell products at the same time when he observed: "Kubrick's crossover success between both mainstream audiences and art house elites speaks to the fact that many of his films were both strong artistic and financial achievements" (Church 2006).

Vincent LoBrutto, author of *Stanley Kubrick: A Biography* and instructor of motion picture editing and film studies for the School of Visual Arts in New York, shared this comparative observation with me on feature films and television commercials:

> Commercial creators, like filmmakers, use the cinematic language that they have learned and see. Kubrick created his own style and movie language that has been embraced by so many. His imagery was distinctive and graphically powerful so others like to use it for their own work. He is one of the greatest filmmakers ever so, like those who borrow and utilize the work of the greatest painters and writers, they go to this.
> (LoBrutto 2018)

Kubrick was himself a pioneer of some ground-breaking advertising campaigns, such as the rapid cut-up style used for *Dr. Strangelove* and *A Clockwork Orange* campaigns, co-developed with Pablo Ferro (Broderick 2017b). In a soon-to-be podcast interview with Pablo Ferro for *Kubrick's Universe* (https://skas.podbean.com) Ferro was asked in October 2017 about his first communication with Kubrick who had sought him out after seeing some of his work in commercial production. "I was shocked," he began. "We sent over the commercials work that I'd done and he called me and he said to come on over, you got a job." Ferro further explained that the *Strangelove* trailer was produced more in the style of the TV commercials of the time, selling consumer products. "He said to me I want you to do a trailer like you sell commercials" (Ferro 2017). To reiterate, as Kubrick said to *Rolling Stone* more than two decades later he observed in some of the best television commercials: "Incredible eight-frame cuts. And you realize that in thirty seconds they've created an impression of something rather complex" (Cahill 1987).

Despite Stanley Kubrick only directing 13 feature films, it seems as though every film from *Spartacus* onwards (perhaps with the exception of *Barry Lyndon*) has taken root to some degree in our collective consciousness. Similarly, elements from Kubrick's work are used over and over by other filmmakers in homage or imitation, as well as television programs, stand-up comedy, news broadcasts, music videos, etc. (Broderick 2017a). The following taxonomy and analysis explores how Kubrick's works have been referenced, mostly in television advertising (or "commercials") and, to a lesser extent, in print media. The films are discussed in order of their relevance and frequency of appearance, often accrued over time as their cultural impact grows, and not necessarily by year of release.

There are now entire product lines, as well as occasional brick and mortar establishments, that have branded themselves after Kubrick in some way. For example there is a soft drink manufacturer in Australia called Strangelove soda.[2] There is a line of Japanese toys called Kubricks.[3] There have been bars in Manhattan, White Plains New York, Austin Texas, and Mexico using Korova or Moloko as a name and/or an interior Korova Milk Bar design motif (Kandel ND). There is also a range of marijuana edibles called Korova.[4] In the past few years billboards displaying these products could be found in the Los Angeles and San Francisco area (Elias 2017). The Korova brand displays a trademark cow wearing a bowler hat and one eye sporting a large eyelash à la Alex DeLarge in *A Clockwork Orange*. Similarly, Canadian Vape manufacturer has a line of Kubrick-inspired products such as Kubrick's Kustard, Horrorshow, A Clockwork Lemon, and more.[5]

One particularly relevant company references several Kubrick films across multiple commercials and even alludes to the filmmaker's iconic work for its name: Monolith Advertising. It appears from their website that they are a fledgling company looking for investors.[6] On their Vimeo page they have more than one ad—essentially video showreels—employing Kubrick motifs.[7] One product is a monolith-shaped machine to be placed in a retail area. The concept is simple. When you chance upon the device in a store you see a mirror image of yourself (actually a real-time video loop of what the machine is seeing and showing back to you). Unlike a mirror, the apparatus is able to add products to the image to instantly show you wearing or holding selected accessories. The video/demo shows a rectangular upright black slab, which is clearly modeled on the *2001* monolith, while playing Shostakovich's "Waltz 2" from *Eyes Wide Shut* over the clip (Birac 2011).

2001: A Space Odyssey

Perhaps not surprisingly the most referenced Kubrick film in advertising is *2001: A Space Odyssey* with *The Shining* in distant second place. However, for the purposes of this essay I would like to set up a definitional distinction. While the film influence is often overt and unambiguous there are times where it becomes more nuanced and contestable. I would define any given commercial "Kubrick-influenced" if there is at least one obvious reference, or two less obvious allusions contained within the same ad.

For example, there are many commercials which simply use Richard Strauss's "Also Sprach Zarathustra," but beyond that there is no overt connection to *2001: A Space Odyssey*. A representative sample includes the 2013 Empire Today flooring ad (Perry 2015), Beef O'Brady (Ad Partners 2017), and Walgreen's 2016 Great Minds commercial (Walgreens 2016). Strauss's majestic tone poem was composed and first performed in 1896. Its gravitas and the significance it conveys (based on Friedrich Nietzsche's novel) is highly effective. It has been used numerous times in many ways. But should the impact and influence of Kubrick's film claim sole credit? This is one of those contentious issues that may never be definitively resolved. Obviously Strauss's music existed and had been performed 72 years before Kubrick adopted it, yet it seems implausible to deny that the April 1968 release of *2001* has catapulted it to a level of familiarity exponentially higher than before. By repeatedly using this musical sequence (Zarathustra's "Introduction," or "Sunrise") both within the film and in its cinema marketing, Kubrick's movie transformed the opening fanfare by Strauss from a late nineteenth-century highbrow score to a popular twentieth-century anthem evoking tremendous power and portent.

When other elements are added to the filmic allusion, the association is arguably stronger. The 2015 St Bernard Septic advertisement (Quinlan 2015), for example, uses the Zarathustra theme but also employs slow motion photography for dramatic effect. *2001* had evoked the same effect during its "Dawn of Man" sequence as well as for much of the zero gravity movement depicted later in the film.[8]

In 2017 Rocket Mortgage crafted two different versions of an advertisement, one with a Caucasian couple and another with an African-American couple. Initially these commercials had no recognizable connection to *2001: A Space Odyssey* until suddenly, at the very end, the couples "blast off" once

Kubrick: tropes in advertising 71

they have their loan approved, segueing to "Also Sprach Zarathustra" while the couples float as if in zero gravity (Quicken Loans 2017a, 2017b). The same year a television spot for Power Tee titled "Golf Odyssey" overlays the Strauss piece while a close-up shows a golf ball slowly rising up into frame like the cresting horizon of a planet (Power Tee 2017). A German company, Bad Reichenhaller, also from 2017 produced a similar effect but with a monolith-like rounded container of salt emerging into the frame (Kubrick's Tube 2017a). These examples demonstrate the lasting legacy of Kubrick's 1968 film having commercial resonance in contemporary popular culture.

Somewhat paradoxically, a 1975 commercial from Mego also used the Zarathustra fanfare to sell *Planet of the Apes* figurines (Mantooth 2006). These movie tie-ins, creatively and temporally, are actually the antithesis of the "Dawn of Man" apes, but regardless of the advert conflating cinematic apes from the future with apes from the past, these ape toys were marketed as thematically connected to *2001*.

Two giants of international sport, Tiger Woods and LeBron James, have both appeared in TV commercials using "Also Sprach Zarathustra" and employing a space theme. A Gatorade ad portrays Tiger Woods in a space suit playing golf on the moon as the Strauss composition is heard before segueing into Norman Greenbaum's "Spirit in the Sky" (Clotheslinemedia 2008). In a commercial for Kia, LeBron James also dons a full space suit and (in one version of the ad) a jazzed up version of "Also Sprach Zarathustra" plays as James enters his Kia for takeoff (Kia 2016). Similarly, an earlier Hyundai automotive ad from 2007 plays "Zarathustra," but while the car is shown as if it were floating in space it adds a harmonic chorus of angelic voices similar to György Ligeti's "Lux Aeterna," a different but familiar piece from the *2001* soundtrack (Bero 2009).

Other notable television commercial allusions to the film include a 1987 ad from British Airways featuring a futuristic space plane with a stewardess returning a floating pen to a passenger (SCAK 2016a); a 1999 Smart Money ad using the HAL9000 character (SCAK 2016c); a Bank of America spot from the same year depicting a monolith style automatic teller machine; and a 2001 HBO promotion featuring excerpts from the "Dawn of Man" sequence (Kubricks Tube 2016b).

Hence, these advertisers have historically adopted a variety of imagery and sounds to evoke metonymical associations with *2001* for space travel, planets, apes, zero gravity, slow motion, the "Dawn of Man", the monolith, and the character of HAL. Others combine some of the above-mentioned aspects, as in the *2001* ad for Pepsi, "Kasparov vs the Machine," which uses both HAL and the monolith (Kalabcin 2006). There are many more television ads directly related to *2001*. In fact I found 60 commercials that I had personally recorded or later discovered while conducting further research, but describing or analyzing these are beyond the scope of the space available here.[9]

Regarding print advertising, some examples include a 2011 ad for the Serbian Film Festival Kustendorf, showing a spaceman with the same red helmet as Dave Bowman aboard the Discovery (Kustendorf 2011). There was also a 2011 promotion for the Adelaide Symphony Orchestra in Australia, which reads "2011: Space Classics" atop an image of an orchestral drummer hitting a bass drum with two large femur bones (Showpony 2011). This second print advertisement cleverly elicits associations with *2001* across both visual and aural dimensions.

From personal memory, albeit not catalogued or recorded in any way, I can attest to the fact that the phrase "A (fill-in-the-blank) Odyssey" was used almost ad nauseam, no pun intended, in both the year 2000 and 2001 in many magazines and newspapers, more often than not as a headline for an article but sometimes in advertisements as well. For example a 2000 *Radio Times* cover page headlined "2001 a TV Odyssey" against a backdrop of a television remote control floating above planet Earth (Radio Times 2001). An October 2000 issue of *Popular Mechanics* featured an article, "2001 A Car Odyssey" (Popular Mechanics 2000) and in late December 2001, the U.K. *Guardian* newspaper ran an article titled "2001: A Political Odyssey" (The Guardian 2001).[10]

The Shining

At the time of finalizing this essay I had discovered 23 television commercials from various parts of the world referencing *The Shining* to promote their products. As with *2001*, such identifications are occasionally contentious but in the case of *The Shining* more often the association is clear. Less obvious would be a Dewar's whiskey commercial featuring the actress Claire Forlani set in a strikingly familiar bar (newschannel365 2013). Even though there is no Lloyd serving Jack a "bourbon and advocaat," the manner in which the set is lit and its use of color bears a strong resemblance to and likely inspiration from the fictional Overlook Hotel's "Gold Room" bar. Another seemingly tangential liquor ad, for Smirnoff, employs sets that evoke the old world opulence of *The Shining*'s hotel (Παναγιώτης Παν 2010). The ad is set on a luxury ship (perhaps the Titanic?) during the early part of the twentieth century but the defining element is the use of "Midnight, the Stars and You" by Ray Noble and Al Bowly (1934), the song that plays as Jack Torrance re-enters the Gold Room and is reprised at the film's conclusion over the enigmatic hotel lobby photo featuring Jack in formal dinner wear on July 4, 1921.

Other commercials seem to leave no question as to the influence of *The Shining*. For example, a British ad for Premier Inn stars comic Lenny Henry. He is shown axing through a door, saying "Heeere's Lenny!" as he squeezes his face through the partial opening. The homage and humor stems from the advert's disclosure that Henry stayed at the wrong motel, thus causing his violent outburst (McFarlane 2010). An older ad for the Sci-Fi Channel from the 1980s employs an almost identical action by the Crypt Keeper character from the television program *Tales From the Crypt* (Kubricks Tube 2016h), whereas the Cartoon Network evokes *The Shining* by showing the Jinxy cartoon character riding his low bike through hotel corridors only to confront *Shining*-like twins (two mice from the same cartoon series) akin to the ghostly Grady girls.

The trope continues in a recent promo for the CNN television show *Quest Means Business*, where presenter Richard Quest maneuvers through a hedge maze to demonstrate the difficulty of navigating the business world (nch 2016). If there was any doubt over *The Shining* allusion, he then makes a turn to discover "twin" girls standing before him, staring ominously. Ubiquitous, creepy twins have also appeared in Cingular's GoPhone ad (CommercialCriticBlog 2009) whereas the Verizon's "Dead Zone" commercial varies the theme by depicting boys of different height who, although clearly not twins, dress identically and appear suddenly in a hallway speaking in ghostly tones (bcut7399 2008).

The popular "Got Milk?" advertising campaign drew from Kubrick's horror film adaptation of the Stephen King novel, and not an ad inspired by *A Clockwork Orange* (which may seem a more appropriate reference), in homage to *The Shining* (Congreso de Publicidad Roastbrief 2015). It contains many stylistic elements from the film, including the use of transition title cards, the twin girls, the hallway, the bike, Danny, and even milk (instead of blood) surging from an elevator all while the child actor playing Danny Torrance repeats in a raspy, Tony-like voice: "Klim Tog," "Klim Tog," i.e. "Got Milk" backwards, playfully gesturing to Danny's memorable "Redrum" vocalization and mirror-inverted text.

Poland's Hotel Bulwar replicated the paean to *The Shining* and Kubrick with a commercial featuring a boy like Danny snaking through the hotel on his tricycle (RawPaw Films 2016). As he approaches a room with a key dangling, highly reminiscent of Danny encountering room 237, the underlying orchestral music we hear throughout is revealed to be diegetic, since the Danny character can hear it too. In fact he is seeking it out as the source of the sound and opens the door to find an orchestra inexplicably in the room playing the music. At the conclusion of the advert the percussionist on the drums assists the boy in striking the drums in a manner that evokes the same notes heard in "Also Sprach Zarathustra," providing a double Kubrick-film referent.

Virtually every commercial employing *Shining* tropes include characters, actions, or motifs drawn from Danny and/or the twins, the axing of a door, or hallways or the tricycle. Refreshingly, a 2014 McDonald's McCafe advertisement avoided all such devices. Instead, the advert shows office co-workers wondering what is occupying the copying machine to the point where an unusually large stack of paper is sitting in the out tray. They pull out one page to reveal the text: "All work and no French Vanilla makes Johnny a dull boy" (McDonalds 2014). Unlike Jack's manic manuscript where the line is continually repeated in varying shapes and form, the McCafe ad uses a single line to make its point yet *The Shining* reference is indisputable.

More recently the 2018 Academy Award ceremony debuted a new TV spot during the broadcast overtly citing *The Shining*. The commercial seemingly promotes the Overlook Hotel as a real destination. It initially portrays the venue as peaceful and bucolic only to show blood being cleaned up, broken doors being inspected, etc. The ad, which includes some original footage from the Kubrick estate, suggests the hotel is being refurbished in preparation for your coming visit with a later revelation that the commercial is actually a promotion for the oft-delayed Academy Museum in Los Angeles. The Kubrick reference is not as arbitrary as it may first seem, since when the Academy Museum opens it will display the Aries 1B Trans-Lunar Space Shuttle used in *2001: A Space Odyssey* (Hammond 2015, Nudd 2018).

In my opinion the two best product commercials ever made using Kubrick tropes emanate from Ikea and Bing, both as overt allusions to *The Shining*. Bing employs the music, the hotel (inside and out), the Danny character (on a bike and also speaking in Tony's voice using his finger), bartender Lloyd, Jack coming through an axed door, and the twins—effectively as much as can be squeezed into a 30 second advert. It is extremely well designed, executed, shot, and edited (Wilber510 2009). The Ikea commercial is nearly three times longer at 83 seconds and portrays the Danny character cycling through a labyrinthine Ikea store (BrainSocial 2014). The ad humorously (self)reflects shoppers' engagement with the Swedish furniture chain and its unusual and confusing layout. "Danny" snakes through the store at such a pace that you can barely see what objects he is passing. But if you look closely (or rewind to watch it "for ever and ever") you can find an astonishing amount of Kubrick film references amongst the 'Easter eggs' discoverable in the commercial. For example, a sign says "redrug," and a large teddy bear suggestively leans over on a bed (alluding to the bizarre encounter Wendy Torrance witnesses amongst Overlook ghosts). Unsurprisingly there are twins. Few commercials can resist paying homage to the twins when spoofing *The Shining*. It remains a masterful television commercial.[11]

Unlike *2001*, mentioned above, only rarely has *The Shining* been used in print advertising outside of marketing efforts to promote the film itself. One interesting exception is an image for VOD (VTR on Demand), which has the tagline "your favorite movie over and over again" while showing an assembly line of bathroom doors, ready for chopping (Grey Agency Network 2016). Another includes Portugal's Oportos Fantastic Film Festival sponsored by Modelos Supermarket. Here *The Shining* twins are standing at the back of a dimly lit supermarket aisle, in a typical Kubrick-style, one-point-perspective composition.[12]

Dr. Strangelove

After *2001* and *The Shining* the TV commercials pool thins out considerably. Yet there remain some notable examples. A Powerade drink advertisement uses the fast-cutting technique employed by Pablo Ferro for the promotion of *Dr. Strangelove* (Kubrick's Tube 2015). The white titles on black background are configured the same as the film trailer. But to eliminate any doubt over Kubrick's influence, the commercial suddenly slows down and uses an actual clip from the black and white film where Strangelove says, "It is not only possible, it is *essential*."

Dr. Strangelove tropes in print advertising are not common, but one overtly references the film in a cheeky and comical manner, in keeping with the film's satirical themes of sex and death. The Lifestyles condoms ad depicts a woman, Slim Pickens style, straddling a huge bomb that is wrapped in a condom with the tag imploring "Cover the Bomb Before it Explodes!" and "Safety always cums first" (Charette 2011).

Spartacus

Just as Powerade managed to do with *Dr. Strangelove*, another commercial inserted an authentic film clip from a Kubrick movie. In a 2007 Pepsi advertisement a brief clip from *Spartacus* is interspersed as cross-cuts between the Romans (portrayed by actors filmed for the commercial) and excerpts of Kirk Douglas and Tony Curtis in the famous and penultimate "*I'm* Spartacus" scene (Nagy 2007). In the Pepsi ad all the characters want the can of drink, which is meant to go to the eponymous title character. A later British ad for Carlsberg beer similarly riffs off this famous scene from *Spartacus* but it is set in a modern office (Carlsberg 2013).

Full Metal Jacket

Replicating this mash-up mode of faux endorsements from bygone film stars, John Wayne, in military uniform, is inserted into a TV commercial for Coors beer (midnightwolf 2010). Using clever digital effects Wayne is shown interacting with R. Lee Ermey who was recorded specifically for his role in the advertisement. The setup is a boot camp scene with Ermey ranting in full-on Sgt. Hartman mode as he encounters Wayne.

Full Metal Jacket's association in print advertising appears mostly, and somewhat predictably, via R. Lee Ermey overtly adopting his Hartmann persona to sell guns or ammunition or promote television programs. One rare departure from the Ermey/Hartman characterization in print was a Canon advertisement displaying an image of its silver Ixus II camera with the tag "Full Metal Jacket" (BDDP Unlimited Paris For Canon 2000). Another variation was in a supplement to *Focus Magazine* that had a cover near identical to the *Full Metal Jacket* poster art (by Philip Castle) of a marine helmet on a white background.[13] The print ad was promoting the magazine's sponsorship of the Ghent Festival in Flanders, Belgium, where the replica helmet design revised Kubrick's film tagline to read: "Born To Watch" (Film Fest Ghent 2006).

In relation to *Full Metal Jacket*, Kubrick had equated the Vietnam War to an advertising campaign when he observed:

> One of the most notable things about the Vietnam War was that it was manipulated in Washington in a kind of *Alice in Wonderland* way by intellectual hawks who tried to fine-tune reality like an advertising agency, constantly inventing new jargon like "kill ratios," "hamlets pacified," and so forth. The light was always at the end of the tunnel.
>
> (Ciment 2003, 243)

Lolita and *A Clockwork Orange*

Given their controversial subject matter it is not surprising that commercials referencing *Lolita* or *A Clockwork Orange* were difficult to find. One subtle *Lolita*-esque ad was produced for MasterCard and shows a nuclear family driving in a car with the only obvious *Lolita* allusion being the use of Nelson Riddle's tune "Lolita Ya Ya" (Kubricks Tube 2016e). An attractive young girl is in the back seat, about the same age as Sue Lyon in the film. Towards the end while the Riddle score continues the father adjusts his rear-view mirror slightly, looking back in the girl's direction and smiles. Naturally this particular shot is open to interpretation, but it did seem more than innocent given the association.

Kubrick: tropes in advertising 77

Two commercials evoking *A Clockwork Orange* are worth mentioning. A 2003 ad from the former British telecommunications company, Orange, has an office marketing team unsuccessfully trying to tease out promotional connections between "clockwork" and "orange" (Inch 2011), which purposely draws more from the film name than any elements within Kubrick's movie. In contrast a 2005 TV spot to promote a play at New Zealand's Silo Theater evokes numerous *A Clockwork Orange* tropes (Kubricks Tube 2016f). It depicts a glamorous event where Beethoven's Ninth Symphony plays in the background, and a small party of people, dressed in formal wear, sip champagne and converse cordially until a spontaneous eruption of violence ensues, including the splattering of blood. The commercial concludes with a title card: "You are cordially invited to an evening of ultraviolence and Beethoven."

Barry Lyndon

As far as I can ascertain *Barry Lyndon* has not featured in any product advertising that meets my definitional criteria, mentioned above. However, as with commercials using "Also Sprach Zarathustra" with no other aspect referencing *2001*, Handel's "Sarabande"—used repeatedly by Kubrick throughout *Barry Lyndon*—has underscored several ads which, nevertheless, appear to have no other obvious connotation of the movie. The fourth-movement (Sarabande) of Handel's Keyboard suite in D minor predates Kubrick's film by more than two centuries which again raises the contentious question—has the filmmaker's use of Sarabande made it more recognizable in contemporary culture? The answer is probably yes but, again, short of a vast qualitative survey the conjecture remains unproven. However, three recent commercials employ the piece, so perhaps this signals part of the recent renaissance and resurgence of interest in *Barry Lyndon*. These comprise a 2002 Levi's jeans commercial (Bluejeans 4e 2013), a 2017 advert for Evony *The King's Return* mobile app game (Evony Mobile 2017), and a Van Houtte coffee advertisement (Van Houtte 2017).

There are also two excellent and related examples of print advertising that play on the poster design of *Barry Lyndon* (Kubrick by Candlelight 2017; Film Offaly 2017). The short film, *Kubrick By Candlelight* (Eire/U.K. 2017, dir: David O'Reilly) has a beautiful print/online ad and promotional poster used for film festivals. Based on the making of *Barry Lyndon* it features actors from the short drama, including a Kubrick character, and places them in the same compositional border frame imitating *Barry Lyndon*'s marketing design depicting several characters posed as if for a painting.

Eyes Wide Shut

Kubrick's last film has influenced television commercials in a number of divergent ways. Nearly two decades after the film's release, some recent adverts depict masked balls or secret societies with clear visual similarities to *Eyes Wide Shut*. Based on Arthur Schnitzler's short 1926 novel, *Traumnovelle*, Kubrick's movie portrayed such clandestine, ritualistic, and orgiastic gatherings, but the filmmaker certainly did not invent the trope. Hence, *Eyes Wide Shut*'s direct influence on (or imitation by) such advertising may be as tenuous as claiming every drill sergeant portrayed in a commercial is a definite nod to *Full Metal Jacket*. Despite this caveat I know from recent observations that the phrase "Eyes Wide Shut party" has been increasingly circulating these past few years. Such popular and idiomatic terminology lends support to the contention that Kubrick's films have a lingering, and growing, impact upon the zeitgeist.

To find a commercial with a more specific reference one of the trailers for the film *2 Fast 2 Furious* (U.S. 2003, dir: John Singleton) opens with the rapper-Actor Ludicrous lyric: "I got my eyes wide shut and my trunk wide open" (Kubricks Tube 2016g). An ad for Campari liquor used "Masked Ball" by Jocelyn Pook, which is featured in *Eyes Wide Shut* (Enchev 2011). This commercial may also have a secondary note of homage in that when the man who has been pursuing a woman catches up to her it reveals he is a woman and she is a man. This may conjure associations with *Eyes Wide Shut* beyond the choice of music, such as the scene where Nick Nightingale is being escorted inside the mansion and Kubrick shows people slow dancing, with a nude man dancing with a clothed man next to a woman dancing with another woman clearly dressed as a man.

Shostakovich's Waltz 2 from his "Jazz Suite," which is essentially the theme to *Eyes Wide Shut*, is used in a Heineken commercial which has no other reference to *Eyes Wide Shut* (TheColevin 2011). But the same piece of music is deployed during a 2017 Lincoln cars advertisement called "Olivia's Wish List" (North Park Lincoln 2017). The ad has two near-identical versions, one of which uses Shostakovich. The only other possible connection to *Eyes Wide Shut*, beyond the choice of song, is that it is a Christmas commercial full of holiday season iconography, similar to the finale of Kubrick's film. Nearly 20 years after its release, advertisers may now be associating *Eyes Wide Shut* with Christmas! In fact the movie was recently chosen by *Esquire* Magazine in 16th position on a list of the 30 Best Christmas Films of all time (Esquire Editors 2017).

In my estimation the best commercial to pay homage to *Eyes Wide Shut* was made in 1999, the year of the film's release. It is for the Lexus GS and features a man driving that car. He douses himself with perfume, smearing lipstick on his shirt, and loosens his tie. During this sequence Chris Isaak's "Baby Did a Bad Thing" is heard. The man arrives home, displaying his disheveled look but his wife mocks him, saying: "Nice try. You've been out driving again." A voice over closes and punctuates the ad with: "Lexus GS; sinful" (Richardson 2016).

Regarding print advertising, a single Sony ad announced their sponsorship of a Kubrick retrospective at a museum in Ghent, Belgium, in 2006 (Sony Center 2006). It presents a couple watching a large Sony television with *Eyes Wide Shut* playing and the top text reads: "Eyes Wide Open."

The Kubrick oeuvre

As mentioned at the beginning of this essay, this analysis does not delve into advertising that directly promotes Kubrick's films or later marketing for such things as Blu-Ray releases. However, I will note that there have been a few accomplished ads that promote either a cable channel or a special program run by a cable channel that mentions Kubrick. One example is the British SkyTV promo series using Anthony Hopkins (TroyDouglas917 2009). In different ads Hopkins makes mention of films he admires, highlighting *The Shining* as one of them. More comprehensive, the Sundance Channel ran a promo for its own Kubrick New Year's mini-marathon (Kubricks Tube 2017b). Over startling bursts of Kubrick imagery an ironically soothing narrator intones "axes . . . horror . . . space child . . . skull crushing . . . ghostly apparitions . . ." as a rapid montage of *2001* and *The Shining* clips bookend loops of Jack Torrance's entering the Gold Room for a New Year's Eve "celebration."

Perhaps the most bizarre commercials in this category are a pair produced for the 2008–2009 Sitges Film Festival in Spain (Lopez 2008, 2009). At the end of the first commercial text appears announcing "2001: A Space Odyssey. 40th Anniversary of a masterpiece that the world didn't appreciate in the beginning." This baffling advertising punchline, however, serves to confirm for the audience a viewing trajectory that commences with bemusement and ends in amusement. The commercial opens with a brown substance spinning, and as it spins it changes shape, but not yet to anything immediately recognizable. Gradually the realization hits; it looks distinctly like excrement. It continues spinning with the "Blue Danube" accompanying in the background and eventually the brown mass begins to assume the shape of a crystal, and ending up as a fully fledged diamond. Yes, the message is clear: *2001: A Space Odyssey* started as a turd and ended up a gem! The second Sitges Film Festival commercial is shot in black and white and depicts a number of people proclaiming (ironically) the reasons they hate *2001*. It concludes with "Si la juzgas solo como una película, puede que te parezca una mierda," which translates to "If you judge it just like a movie, it may seem like shit."

In 2017 Universal Studios obtained the rights to use content from *The Shining* for their annual Halloween Horror Nights attractions in both Los Angeles and Orlando. Universal promoted the events widely with some creative commercials that interweave tropes from not just *The Shining* but from other screen entertainments, such as *American Horror Story* and *Saw* (Horror Night Junkie 2017). I was fortunate to sight a promotional billboard on a highway in Orlando advertising this event and to my surprise the sign said "Stanley Kubrick's The Shining" making it the only ad I have found where the name Kubrick is visible in product promotion, except for direct advertising by Kubrick's own production associates (Marinaccio 2017).

Possibly the finest advertisement referencing Kubrick was created within this category. The 2008 British Channel Four commercial promoting a "Kubrick Season" was unparalleled (acrossthepondwebsite 2008). In a glorious single-take, eye-level, point-of-view dolly shot, the camera weaves through a recreated studio backstage displaying aspects of the filming of *The Shining*. Much like the previously cited Ikea commercial this one needs to be viewed several times in order to notice all the details. Channel Four went to extraordinary lengths to replicate the look of the film, to the point that they even cast an actress who looked exactly like June Randall, Kubrick's long-time continuity manager, who appears momentarily at the end holding a document and says direct to camera: "Your script, Mr. Kubrick." The comment and gesture at this point makes it obvious to the viewer that the elaborate P.O.V. belonged to Kubrick (and we as audience/spectator, by assuming the position of the camera-eye).[14]

An unintended legacy?

Although not directly related to Kubrick tropes in advertising, I would like to share one final observation. Although highly speculative it concerns the possibility that some commercials may have unintentionally undermined a widespread Kubrickian influence on mainstream Anglo-American culture and the English-speaking world. To establish this thesis let me first reaffirm that the year *two-thousand-and-one* (said in that particular fashion) has been spoken this way and heard innumerably since the film's release in 1968. Kubrick and Arthur C. Clarke had specifically discussed whether or not to pronounce "2001" as either *two-thousand-and-one* or *twenty-oh-one*, an exchange personally confirmed for me by Kubrick's daughter, Katharina. Once Kubrick and Clarke agreed on the vocalization, the impact of the film's title quickly assumed a colloquial register that remained right up to the advent of the new millennium some 32 years later.[15]

When the calendar turned to 2000, no-one said *twenty-oh-oh* or, as with 1900, *twenty-hundred*, because it sounded awkward. Everyone said *two thousand*. The next year, even though billions of English-speakers could have switched to saying *twenty-oh-one*, virtually everyone maintained the Kubrick-Clarke utterance of *two-thousand-and-one*. The pronunciation continued for most of that decade, although I do recall a modicum of contrarians who would say *twenty-oh-three*, *twenty-oh-four*, etc. It was a topic very few deliberated, it all just seemed to evolve organically.

I had predicted to myself that the tide would shift in 2010 with more people changing to the shorter pronunciation. Around the Fall of 2009 I heard a commercial for a car manufacturer announcing: "the new twenty ten Hondas are out." That moment I semi-seriously said to myself: "it's official, once it's in a commercial it is official." In general, advertising doesn't start trends, they conspicuously follow and imitate trends and through repetition validate them (Nudd 2016). By 2010 there was a huge shift in people pronouncing that year in the shortened form, specifically *twenty-ten* and not *two thousand and ten*. While these are unscientific observations and largely anecdotal, it did occur to me that once television commercials began repeating "twenty-ten" there was a sea change in how people began to pronounce those years of the second decade of the twenty-first century.

In conclusion, from the above analysis and my final comments, it seems unimpeachable to me that Kubrick's films have had, and continue to have, an enormous influence on advertising and many other fields.[16] As I have outlined, advertisers frequently tap into the public's familiarity with Kubrick film tropes to evoke associations of awe, wonder, and humor. Prominent amongst these are repetitions and variations on the monolith, the Grady twins, the Dawn of Man apes, the vicious drill instructor, as well as "classic" music excerpted from *Lolita* through to *Eyes Wide Shut*. Many other motifs are recycled across a wide array of television commercials and print advertisements in America, Britain, and elsewhere.

Considering Kubrick's broad influences the history of advertising offers, and will continue to offer, a great array of work to dissect. I am reminded that Kubrick himself enjoyed similar detailed observations and engaged in such critical dissection. Director and long-time friend of Kubrick, Sydney Pollack, who also acted in *Eyes Wide Shut*, recalled soon after Kubrick's death: "I remember once we got into a discussion over there being too many words in English dialogue. So he started taping NesCafe commercials. At the time in France there were these NesCafe commercials that were basically mini-dramas. So Stanley would send me these little NesCafe commercials [. . .] and he would edit them! Then he would say, 'Now, there were 93 words in this and I took 17 of them out' (Ingui 2004).

82 *James Marinaccio*

How immutable are these Kubrickian references and homages? Only time will tell. Regardless, despite a great deal of research, I have undoubtedly missed identifying many older commercials which would require enormous resources to locate, especially those in print. And, naturally, there are sure to be many more Kubrick-inspired adverts produced well into the future. So, viddy well consumers.

Notes

1. See for example Peter Krämer 2013, "'To prevent the present heat from dissipating': Stanley Kubrick and the Marketing of *Dr. Strangelove* (1964)." *InMedia*. No.3. https://journals.openedition.org/inmedia/634
2. For examples, see www.strangelove.com.au/
3. Examples of the range of toys can be found at www.medicomtoystore.com/kubrickcollectio.html
4. For examples of these marijuana edibles, see www.korovaedibles.com/. Although these names stem from the novel by Anthony Burgess, it was Kubrick's 1972 film adaptation that has had the more considerable influence on public memory.
5. Vape examples can be found at https://reduxvapers.com/collections/juice-by-kubrick
6. For examples, see http://monolithadvertising.com/
7. See Martin Birac's website: https://vimeo.com/user5238272
8. The latter is not, technically, slow motion but appears as such.
9. Readers interested in exploring this theme can access my Kubrick blog (http://kubrickarticles.blogspot.com/2017/12/blog-post.html) and a YouTube channel featuring many of the TV commercials discussed in this chapter (www.youtube.com/user/TheJnatch).
10. For further examples, the following link displays many print ads and sundry Kubrick advertising material (https://postimg.ccgallery/1156556hq).
11. The director of the Ikea ad was Scott McClelland who was chosen as *Creativity Magazine*'s top 50 most creative people for 2014. Under the corporate umbrella came Creativity Magazine, AdCritic.com, and the *Madison & Vine* newsletter, all no longer in press. I worked at *Creativity* magazine myself from 2001–2004 as circulation marketing manager in the Ad Age Group of products. That term, clearly melding the worlds of entertainment film and the advertising world, was a phrase coined by then editor of *Ad Age*, Scott Donaton, who said in his 2004 book of the same name: "When done right, product integration can enhance both a brand's image and the entertainment experience." See: https://adage.com/article/viewpoint/excerpt-book-madison-vine/40494/
12. Examples of Kubrick's legendary one-point perspective can be seen here: https://creators.vice.com/en_au/article/8qm3pa/stanley-kubrick-one-point-perspective-supercut-is-the-latest-in-a-series-exploring-filmmaking-tropes
13. For examples of Philip Castle's artwork for *Full Metal Jacket*, see: www.designcurial.com/news/airbrushing-history-4159971/
14. The commercial was directed by Siri Bunford who won the "Yellow Pencil" at the D&AD Awards as well as the BTA Diploma award. See: www.freethebid.com/directors/siri-bunford/

15 The Kubrick-Clarke pronunciation enabled decades of "adequate preparation and conditioning," as Heywood Floyd says to the specialists gathered at the security briefing on the American moon base at Clavius.
16 To reiterate, the advertising described here is not a complete list. For television ads alone I found over 100 but due to space restrictions could not mention many of them. Hence, the chapter is not a greatest hits list. In terms of companies and products most associated with Kubrick film tropes, Apple had the most with four advertisements. Pepsi and the Sitges Film Festival had three each, and seven other companies/brands had two television commercials each.

Works cited

acrossthepondwebsite. 2008. "The Stanley Kubrick Season More4 Promo." July 10. www.youtube.com/watch?v=x_dYUH5ji0w.

Ad Partners Advertising Agency. 2017. "Beef 'O'Brady's 3X the Premium Burger & Nashville Hot Wings!" January 4. www.youtube.com/watch?v=vUL7i_30Xw4.

antasporto. 2008. "Miudas." March 8. http://onossoportfolio.blogspot.com/2008/03/.

bcut7399. 2008. "Verizon Dead Zones- Freaky Brothers." September 5. www.youtube.com/watch?v=2QrlEYNfODI.

BDDP Unlimited Paris for Canon. 2000. "Full Metal Jacket Canon." June 1. www.coloribus.com/adsarchive/prints/canon-ixus-ii-full-metal-jacket-2294555/.

Bero, Brian. 2009. "Hyundai DUH." September 29. www.youtube.com/watch?v=DgP2T1BfrzE.

Birac, Martin. 2011. "Monolith-Reality Augmented Advertising Machine." November 27. https://vimeo.com/31742087.

Bluejeans 4e. 2013. "Levi's 2002 Odyseey (Haendel—Sarabande)." August 20. www.youtube.com/watch?v=yNFUS05I-aw.

BrainSocial. 2014. "IKEA Halloween Ad." October 23. www.youtube.com/watch?v=5M9HWST_HMg.

Broderick, Mick. 2017a. "Post-Kubrick: On the Filmmaker's Influence and Legacy." *Screening the Past*, no. 42. www.screeningthepast.com/2017/09/post-kubrick-on-the-filmmakers-influence-and-legacy/.

———. 2017b. "Animating Kubrick—Auteur Influences in *The Simpsons*." *Screening the Past*, no. 42. www.screeningthepast.com/2017/09/animating-kubrick-auteur-influences-in-the-simpsons/.

Cahill, Tim. 1987. "The Rolling Stone Interview: Stanley Kubrick." *The Rolling Stone*, August 27. www.rollingstone.com/movies/movie-news/the-rolling-stone-interview-stanley-kubrick-in-1987-90904/.

Carlsberg. 2013. "Carlsberg 'Spartacus.'" February 15. www.youtube.com/watch?v=CsRFlJ7lqJg.

Charette, Emily. 2011. "Dr. Strangelove—Lifestyle Condom Ad." April 6. https://emilycharette.wordpress.com/2011/04/06/dr-strangelove-lifestyles-condom-ad.

Church, David. 2006. "The Cult of Kubrick." *Off-screen* 10, no. 5. https://offscreen.com/view/cult_kubrick.

Ciment, Michel. 2003. *Kubrick: The Definitive Edition*. London: Faber & Faber.

Clotheslinemedia. 2008. "Tiger Woods Gatorade Moon Shot Commercial." March 22. www.youtube.com/watch?v=Mp4n2Wuczl0.
CommercialCriticBlog. 2009. "Cingular Go Phone Commercial 'Horror.'" June 24. www.youtube.com/watch?v=jqWYxT6oD0g.
Congreso de Publicidad Roastbrief. 2015. "'The Shining' Got Milk Commercial." February 19. www.youtube.com/watch?v=Hxy7gUrzDGw.
Croteau, David, and William Hoynes. 2000. *Media Society: Industries, Images, and Audiences.* Thousand Oaks, CA: Pine Forge.
Elias, Thomas. 2017. "Column: Cannabis Billboard Rules Aim to Protect Children." *The Cannifornian,* February 11. www.thecannifornian.com/cannabis-news/law/column-cannabis-billboard-rules-aim-protect-children/.
Enchev, Damian. 2011. "The Best Campari Ad." March 26. www.youtube.com/watch?v=bFCk_tXlDpY.
Esquire Editors. 2017. "The 30 Best Christmas Movies of All Time." November 21. www.esquire.com/entertainment/movies/a50565/best-christmas-movies-of-all-time/.
Evony Mobile. 2017. "The Battle of Evony—BIG GAME Commercial—Extended Cut." February 4. www.youtube.com/watch?v=aAO1YesuVik.
Ferro, Pablo. 2017. Recorded/Unreleased interview by Stephen Rigg for *Kubrick's Universe* podcast. https://skas.podbean.com.
Film Fest Ghent. 2006. "##rd Flanders Film Festival—Ghent Focuses on Stanley Kubrick." September 27. www.filmfestival.be/en/news/33rd-flanders-film-festival-ghent-focuses-on-stanley-kubrick/27-09-2006/200.
Film Offaly. 2017. "Kubrick by Candlelight." September 13. https://s6.postimg.cc bjtsl40rl/kbc2.jpg.
Grey Agency Network. 2016. "VTR on Demand the Shining." May 19. www.adsoftheworld.com/media/print/vtr_on_demand_the_shining.
The Guardian. 2001. "2001: A Political Odyssey." December 17. www.theguardian.com/politics/2001/dec/17/politicalnews.uk.
Hammond, Pete. 2015. "Academy Museum Buys Rare '2001: A Space Odyssey' Model for $344,000." *Deadline.com,* March 29. http://deadline.com/2015/03/academy-museum-spending-344-000-2001-a-space-odyssey-model-1201400763/.
Horror Night Junkie. 2017. "Halloween Horror Nights TV Spot with Directed by Eli Roth | HHN 27 Commercial." August 24. www.youtube.com/watch?v=AiPSs-IsuGU.
Inch, Iain. 2011. "(03) Orange Ad—a Clockwork Orange." May 22. www.youtube.com/watch?v=4ZfptMHpe-o.
Ingui, Chris. 2004. "Recalling Kubrick." *The Hatchet,* April 8. www.gwhatchet.com/2004/04/08/recalling-kubrick/.
Kalabcin. 2006. "Kasparov vs Machine Pepsi Commercial." December 17. www.youtube.com/watch?v=cUqXr9Jlhwc.
Kandel, Erin N. D. "Korova Milk Bar." *New York Magazine.* Accessed December 16, 2017. http://nymag.com/listings/bar/korova_milk_bar/.
Kia. 2016. "Spaceship." *iSpot.tv.* www.ispot.tv/ad/AqyQ/2016-kia-k900-spaceship-featuring-lebron-james.

Krämer, Peter. 2013. "'To Prevent the Present Heat from Dissipating': Stanley Kubrick and the Marketing of *Dr. Strangelove* (1964)." *InMedia*, no. 3. https://journals.openedition.org/inmedia/634.
Kubrick by Candlelight. 2017. "Encounters Official Selection 2017." https://postimg.ccimage/9sa0hxoj1/.
Kubricks Tube. 2015. "Powerade Ad Like Dr Strangelove Trailer." November 6. www.youtube.com/watch?v=43Fuzo8C5_c.
———. 2016a. "British Airways TV Commercial Approx 1987 Spoofs 2001: A Space Odyssey." June 14. www.youtube.com/watch?v=pEe0c9PTXdk.
———. 2016b. "HBO Dawn of Man (2001) TV Spot." June 14. www.youtube.com/watch?v=WUGVbSW0i9w.
———. 2016c. "Smartmoney Commercial from @ 1999 Spoofs 2001: A Space Odyssey." June 5. www.youtube.com/watch?v=2KMRsvnSsN4.
———. 2016d. "Bank of America 2001 ad Summer 2002." May 29. www.youtube.com/watch?v=QYdChLhQjVk.
———. 2016e. "MasterCard 'Lolita' Inspired TV Commercial." June 5. www.youtube.com/watch?v=-ILr8ZYnq_Y.
———. 2016f. "Silo Theatre a Clockwork Orange Production Posh Party Film 59099 Adeevee." December 9. www.youtube.com/watch?v=763aT1QD9Dk.
———. 2016g. "2Fast2Furioustrailer Eyes Wide Shut." December 6. www.youtube.com/watch?v=WiPFB-Decd0.
———. 2016h. "Sci Fi Channel Promo Spoofs the Shining (approx 1992)." June 14. www.youtube.com/watch?v=saQEcqhHp0g.
———. 2017a. "Bad Reichenhaller Salz Marken Jodsalz (salt) TV Commercial." June 12. www.youtube.com/watch?v=IwE67mO0cK8.
———. 2017b. "Sundance Channel New Year's Eve Kubrick Festival TV Ad." February 11. www.youtube.com/watch?v=PT3CpVXV6FE&feature=youtu.be.
Kustendorf Film and Music Festival. 2011. "Odyssey Kustendorf 2011." January 5. www.kustu.com/w2/en:kuestendorf_film_music_festival.
Lopez, Christian. 2008. "Ad Sitges Kubrick' 08." October 22. www.youtube.com/watch?v=gkyllSvOhZU.
———. 2009. "Made at Home: Ad Sitges Kubrick' 08." April 16. www.youtube.com/watch?v=-1G8jUg61Q0.
Mantooth, Brick. 2006. "Mego Planet of the Apes Dolls Commercial." May 22. www.youtube.com/watch?v=objzif2dW7g.
Marinaccio, James. 2017. "Photo_taken_on_Highway_528_Orlando_September_26_2017." *PostImage*, September 26. https://s6.postimg.cckz1ut2t5t/Photo_taken_on_Highway_528_Orlando_September_26_2017.jpg.
McDonalds. 2014. "Johnny." *iSpot.tv*. www.ispot.tv/ad/7piG/mcdonalds-mccafe-iced-coffee-johnny.
McFarlane, Grant. 2010. "Premier Inn Advert." August 19. www.youtube.com/watch?v=qm3kVw7b0ZE.
midnightwolf. 2010. "Coors Light Commercial with R Lee Ermey." December. www.youtube.com/watch?v=5E3TA7kvzQY&t=1s mjs269. 2011.
"Old Pepsi Commercial." September 22. www.youtube.com/watch?v=6CGoYy9_Ibw.

Nagy, Mohamed. 2007. "Hilarious Pepsi Advertisement (Spartacus Version)." July 11. www.youtube.com/watch?v=-FYGmMzwJRA.

nch. 2016. "CNN International 'Quest Means Business Promo." July 26. www.youtube.com/watch?v=q1ida8WCFBc.

newschannel365. 2013. "Claire Forlani Sexes Up Whisky Ads." June 6. www.youtube.com/watch?v=aki_ohB6g00.

Noble, Ray and Al Bowly. 1934. "Midnight, the Stars and You". New York: RCA Victor Company.

North Park Lincoln. 2017. "Lincoln Presents—Olivia's Wish List." November 21. www.youtube.com/watch?v=XdfkIFMwKQw.

Nudd, Tim. 2016. "The Year in Creativity: 20 Trends that Drove Some of 2016's Best Marketing." *AdWeek*, December 12. www.adweek.com/creativity/year-creativity-20-trends-drove-some-2016s-best-marketing-175052/.

———. 2018. "Why the Overlook Hotel from The Shining Got an Ad on the Oscars." *AdWeek*, March 4. www.adweek.com/creativity/why-the-overlook-hotel-from-the-shining-got-an-ad-on-the-oscars/.

Olenski, Steve. 2012. "What Makes a Television Commercial Memorable and Effective?" *Forbes.com*, October 19. www.forbes.com/sites/marketshare/2012/10/19/what-makes-a-tv-commercial-memorable-and-effective/#4102c7fb3079.

Openculture.com. 2013. "Watch the First Commercial Ever Shown on American TV" August 2. www.openculture.com/2013/08/watch-the-first-commercial-ever-shown-on-american-tv-1941.html.

Perry, Catherine. 2015. "Empire Flooring: 50/50/50 Sale TV Commercial." March 3. www.youtube.com/watch?v=tIgca5GPLoc.

Popular Mechanics. 2000. "Automotive 2001: A Car Odyssey." October 1. https://books.google.co.ck/books?id=OXYo4mrq9Q4C&pg=PA82&source=gbs_toc_r&cad=2#v=onepage&q&f=false.

Power Tee. 2017. "Golf Odyssey." *iSpot.tv*. www.ispot.tv/ad/wReK/power-tee-golf-odyssey-song-by-keith-merrill.

Quicken Loans. 2017a. "Rocket Mortgage Makes Getting a Home Loan Easy." January 27. www.youtube.com/watch?v=KpRSiy2fOpU.

———. 2017b. "Rocket Mortgage Helps You Get a Home Loan Fast." January 27. www.youtube.com/watch?v=40v-GVbV_jI.

Quinlan, Matt. 2015. "Total Septic Commercial with St. Bernard—2015." December 7. www.youtube.com/watch?v=Ot5SIHsbc74.

Radio Times. 2001. "New Season Special." January 6. www.pinterest.com/pin/165788830010318495.

RawPaw Films. 2016. "Hotel Bulwar—MFF Tofifest 2015." March 13. www.youtube.com/watch?v=Z3BBOm0qWmo.

Richardson Keith. 2016. "Lexus GS Commercial 1999." September 19. www.youtube.com/watch?v=Ym47TnEqb_4.

Showpony Advertising. 2011. "Space Classics. Adelaide Symphony Orchestra." *Greymatter Collective*, August 19. www.greymattercollective.com/print-advertising-adelaide-symphony-orchestra-space-classics-showpony/.

Sony Center. 2006. "Eyes Wide Open." May 10. https://postimg.ccimage/inausevb1/.
Stockfelt, Ola. 2010. "Book Review: Music in Advertising. Commercial Sounds in Media Communication and Other Settings." *MedieKultur: Journal of Media and Communication Research*, no. 48: 145–47.
TheColevin. 2011. "Heineken Commercial." July 29. www.youtube.com/watch?v=mFcKKh6XfTw
TroyDouglas917. 2009. "Anthony Hopkins on 'The Shining.'" August 17. www.youtube.com/watch?v=2uztxXBTavA.
Van Houtte. 2017. "Van Houtte® Ad—Become a Master with Van Houtte®—EN—30s." October 20. www.youtube.com/watch?v=X1ZhXhY6p7I.
Walgreens. 2016. "Great Minds." *iSpot.tv*. www.ispot.tv/ad/AxWG/walgreens-great-minds.
Wilber510. 2009. "Bing.com Commercial (The Shining Spoof)." November 8. www.youtube.com/watch?v=zTkETDkKXP4.
wtcvidman. 2011. "1990 Oatmeal Crisp & Oatmeal Raisin Crisp Commercial with Anthony Perkins as Norman Bates." October 27. www.youtube.com/watch?v=c6s5DjcLWUI.
Παναγιώτης Παν. 2010. "SMIRNOFF Vodka—Old Commercial." June 1. www.youtube.com/watch?v=VWlpufwiYME.

7 Kubrick on screen

Mick Broderick

This chapter examines the status and evolution of Kubrick's public persona by comparing such perceptions with his limited, official screen appearances. These were either conscious or coincidental acts of public documentation and are contrasted with the quasi-fictional representations of Kubrick as a screen 'character,' principally in feature-length dramas, e.g. *Stranger's Kiss* (1983), *The Life and Death of Peter Sellers* (2004), and *Colour Me Kubrick* (2005).

Such was the enigma of Stanley Kubrick that until the 1980 release of the documentary *Making 'The Shining'* very few critics, let alone fans, had even heard his voice (Combs 1996).[1] Although his face was seen in numerous newspaper and magazine articles over the years (e.g. *Look* 1949, *The Detroit Free Press* 1953, *Playboy* 1968), with his bearded countenance gracing the covers of *The Saturday Review* (1971) and *Newsweek* (1972) and on some more arcane magazine covers (including a 1955 issue of *Chess Life*, and film industry/review magazines such as *American Cinematographer* [1980] and *Monthly Film Bulletin* [1984]), he remained largely 'unrecognized.'[2]

By carefully guarding and limiting his public appearances Kubrick was, paradoxically, unable to influence the entrenched perception of his public persona and was widely regarded as a recluse. From the late 1960s onward he was seldom seen on screen and generally not recognized in public, which only served to heighten the mystique and intrigue surrounding the filmmaker at a time when American auteurs were being catapulted to "superstar" status. As Tom Cruise narrates during the opening sequence of *Stanley Kubrick: A Life in Pictures* (Dir: Jan Harlan 2001), Kubrick was "intensely private, shunning publicity and fiercely guarding his anonymity." This posture was partly in response to Kubrick's concern over personal and familial safety. At the time he and co-writer Arthur C. Clarke were developing *2001* (circa 1965) Clarke noted the filmmaker carried a "large hunting knife in his briefcase" just in case Kubrick had to ward-off a "psychotic" fan stalking him nearby (Benson 2018, 92). A few years later, with controversial allegations of "copy-cat" violence following the release of *A Clockwork Orange*, Kubrick retreated further from the public gaze. Having received numerous death threats, he convinced Warner Brothers to withdraw the film from distribution in Britain (Kubrick 2012).[3] Similarly, the filming of *Barry Lyndon* was abandoned in Ireland after more than one serious threat was made, ostensibly by the I.R.A., against the production and personnel. Kubrick and his family promptly returned to the U.K. with the cast and crew soon following (Barter 2013; Ghosh 2013).[4]

Documenting Stanley

The posthumous, valedictory documentary *Stanley Kubrick: A Life in Pictures* (*LiP*) opens with a rapid montage, whimsically syncopated to Rossini's "Thieving Magpie," where key words from numerous press clippings are highlighted (some repeatedly):

> obsessive perfectionist . . . mysterious person . . . eccentric . . . megalomaniac . . . reclusive . . . demented . . . controlling . . . controversial . . . meticulous . . . controversial . . . hermetic . . . demanding . . . tyranny . . . subversive . . . phobia . . . audacious . . . legend . . .

Tom Cruise's off-camera narration foregrounds the film's agenda as a "document about a man who remained silent whether he was being applauded or damned."

LiP reveals the earliest yet seen film of Stanley Kubrick, taken by his father Jack in the late 1930s. Brief home movie sequences show Stanley with his younger sister, Barbara, on roller skates at an outdoor playing field; together on a park slide; leaning up against a brick wall, laughing; and indoors with the pair dancing rambunctiously. In these silent film snippets the young Kubrick certainly plays to the camera and is visibly aware of its presence. In one sequence Stanley deliberately lets go of his sister, six years his junior, who falls off her skates as he continues to look at the camera and exits the frame to camera left. In another scene, as the siblings dance, Barbara is purposefully bumped to the floor by Stanley's gyrating hip thrust. How Jack Kubrick responded to these pranks is not shown. Perhaps they were 'performed' under his direction, but Stanley seems to be deliberately acting in a manner to elicit some kind of reaction. Not long after her brother's death, Barbara reflected on Stanley rarely being described as "playful." He was, she says, but then demurs: "in the *Addams Family* kind of 'playful'," suggesting that his fraternal demeanor was tinged with capriciousness and sibling jealousy.

90 *Mick Broderick*

Other home movie sequences from the era show Kubrick laying on the floor as Barbara roughly brushes and pulls at his thick dark hair, or the pair of them seated together in profile at an upright piano, with Stanley in focus in the background stroking the ivory keys. Barbara continues: "when he was little I think they did consider him a bit of a sissy because . . . he wasn't like your typical boy; he read a lot, he always had a book." Asked whether her parents were strict in relation to Stanley's upbringing, Barbara is unequivocal: "No, never. He always did what he wanted." Despite these observations, each clip portrays both children as happy and cheerful, smiling and laughing. A brief color scene taken in summer shows Barbara and pre-teen Stanley outdoors in a tight group shot, waving at the camera, with Stanley hugging his mother, Gerty. This contrasts with a similar extended family composition (in black and white) presenting Stanley in a shirt and tie, wearing knickerbockers, and holding a baseball bat, framed alongside his sister, mother, and friends who push a pram down a borough street.

While these home movie scenes are intrinsically amateurish in execution and pedestrian in composition and content, this aesthetic is fundamental to their charm. In contrast with their insertion into the expert artifice of the polished feature documentary, the unaffected 'naturalism' of the clips' presentation remains refreshing some eight decades later. These shots are not to be read as *cinema verité* but conscious acts of recording familial intimacies using a technology few residents of the Bronx in the 1930s would have had the resources to own (camera and projector), let alone undertake expensive film processing. At that time the novelty and allure of home movies would have been both unusual and privileged (Brosnahan 2017).

The inherently retrospective status of home movies (Zimmerman 2008) capturing Stanley Kubrick and his family in casual encounters encourages the observer to reappraise, or reconfirm, commonly held beliefs concerning the filmmaker's personality and deportment. Later material shot by Peter Sellers (or possibly his friend Graham Stark) at Sellers' Chipperfield home (circa 1962) is equally informative. The amateur footage shows Stanley and wife Christiane playing tennis with producer-partner James B. Harris at the time of filming *Lolita*. It is illuminating for its naturalism and display of cultural convention. Whereas Harris plays in an open neck shirt with rolled up sleeves, Kubrick is shown holding his wooden racket, and somewhat incongruously wearing a lightly crumpled dark jacket, shirt, and tie. Though relaxed and smiling, the image nevertheless confirms the repeated descriptions of the artist's lack of sartorial savvy, from his formative teenage apprenticeship as a *Look* photographer to his appearances on-set during *Eyes Wide Shut*.

Other home movies in *LiP* depict Kubrick as both subject *and* filmmaker. In one humorous extract (circa 1970), Stanley films his daughters Anya and Vivian who are seated at an upright piano, an echo of his own father's composition some three decades earlier. However, this scene has sound and records the unseen/off-camera Kubrick challenging his daughters over their "performance." Anya is positioned closer to the camera with Vivian alongside to her left. Kubrick asks: "Do you *often* find me in a temper?" The girls reply in unison with a drawn out "Yeees!"

SK: Oh, I don't believe that . . . I can't believe that.
VK: Well, you better believe it 'cos you just went into a temper a couple of minutes ago.
AK: Yeah, because you can't do this stupid film, because everyone giggles...
SK: I think I . . .
VK: [interrupting]: And because I can't [pounding on the keyboard, in exaggeration] play like that!
SK: I think I'm one of the ni . . . most even tempered people you'll ever meet.

"Ha!" Anya replies, incredulous, lifting her head and rolling her eyes.

A black and white clip from around the same period has Kubrick joking to someone off-camera, possibly Jan Harlan. Ten-year-old daughter Anya sits on his right knee and behind him Vivian is bottle-feeding an infant while Christiane appears to be helping another child (her nephew?) to paint at a garden table. Kubrick says to Anya, pointing at the lens:

SK: Do you know what type of camera that is? What it's called?
AK: [Anya pauses]: It's . . . a home movie . . .
SK: 'Arriflex,' it's called.

Another clip shows Anya on a children's merry-go-round trying to remove a little blonde boy, previously seen painting at the table. Kubrick yells at his daughter "Get 'im off Anya," followed immediately by the more irate command: "Anya, get 'im off. We're *shooting*!" Anya turns away from the carousel and looks at her dad (behind the camera), protesting: "I'm *trying* to!"

These private, slice-of-life portrayals do not shy away from what Anya later described as her father's propensity for "being bossy and too impatient, and putting his director's hat on in an inappropriate way." Kubrick's strictness has also been noted by his eldest daughter, Katharina, who maintains because she was oldest she suffered the most over-protectiveness when it came to boys, while the younger girls later "got away with murder" (Kubrick 2014). These observations, however, are largely tempered by the family's effusive praise of Kubrick's paternal love and care and kindness.

By the early to mid-1970s Kubrick was enveloped in a growing media myth, one that began to increasingly depict him as obsessive, controlling, eccentric, and reclusive to the point where by 1998 *Punch* magazine called him "a barking loon," claiming that "We're hearing stories that Kubrick is even more insane than psychiatrists led us to believe" (Simpson 2008, 235). There is some unfortunate irony in this development since Kubrick took umbrage at others receiving undue credit beyond what he perceived to be creatively fair—usually by collaborators failing to correct or refute the inflated claims of third parties, such as publicists and marketers promoting Terry Southern's singular *Strangelove* contribution. Hence, the filmmaker's deliberate, self-imposed silence on most matters concerning his persona was partly to blame for their continued exaggeration. Over the decades Kubrick's consistent failure to rebut or rebuff the spurious claims, endlessly repeated by journalists looking for a 'hook' or an 'angle,' ultimately fueled and exacerbated the growing, mostly unchallenged, public perception.

Far from the neurotic hermit the media perpetually presented him to be, colleagues, relatives, friends, and collaborators have consistently described Kubrick as a caring husband, a family man devoted to his children, an animal lover, and a convivial host with a sardonic, often risqué, sense of humor. Contrary to popular belief, the "world came to Stanley." Wherever he lived and worked (New York, California, Germany, Spain, London, Ireland) invited guests would be afforded considerable time and generous hospitality. For example, in the 1960s, during the relative calm of project development, Stanley and Christiane would entertain a myriad of guests in their rented Manhattan or central London apartments. The later residences at Abbotts Mead and Childwickbury in England were only a short drive or train trip from both London's CBD and nearby film studios, making him easily accessible to those whom he *wished* to meet. Kubrick would also on occasion drive to the shops, take in a movie or a meal, and interact, incognito, with storekeepers (such as stationers) and purchase goods.

Beyond this extant home movie footage, official non-fiction film of Kubrick can be found in newsreels. Glimpses of the director are evident at the U.K. premiere of *Spartacus*, though he is largely overshadowed by the presence of producer and star, Kirk Douglas. Across scenes of British bobbies forming a cordon to hold back gawking public onlookers, Fred Maness narrates the Universal-International newsreel "London Ovation: Princess Meg attends 'Spartacus' Premiere," describing the film's international debut as "the most brilliant event on London's show business calendar for the year." On the pavement out front of the cinema an elderly couple stand before a chauffeured limousine: "Among the many outstanding dignitaries present is Mrs. Pandit, Prime Minster Nehru's sister and High Commissioner in London." At the very moment this narration commences, as tuxedoed guests arrive and turn to the look at the cine camera, from screen right Stanley Kubrick appears wearing a dark overcoat and reaches into his left breast pocket, presumably for a lighter to ignite the cigarette dangling from his mouth. This accidental coverage of Kubrick captures the highly experienced director-photographer unwittingly blocking the camera's line of sight to the professed "dignitaries." As the segment's title suggests, it is the arrival of Princess Margaret and her husband that garners most attention. "Radiant in a black gown [and] a snowy ermine cape," the royal couple meet a line of bowing and curtsying movie VIPs, including Douglas and his wife. Wearing a tuxedo and standing beside the star-producer is "director Stanley Kubrick," shown in a tight close-up alongside the president of United International Pictures. As with most individual newsreel stories, the segment is taut and zestfully presented, running less than two minutes.

Kubrick was featured two years later in the British Pathé newsreel "Lights! Cameras! Premiere in Manhattan" arriving at the New York premiere of *Lolita*. Michael Fitzmaurice narrates:

> Broadway at dusk, and as the lights go on the *News of the Day* camera records the welcome for *Lolita*. The movie the whole town's talking about. At the gala invitational premiere [. . .] there's acclaim in the film world for director Stanley Kubrick, arriving with Mrs. Kubrick.

The Kubricks are filmed exiting their limo in the rain, with ushers holding umbrellas and sporting comical *Lolita*-esque sunglasses. Wearing a tux and bow-tie, the director turns to the camera and smiles, a cigarette wedged between his lips. There is no exegetic sound or additional commentary about the filmmaker, just further narration about the film, its stars, and its controversy.

Nothing has publicly emerged to date of Kubrick on screen at the time of *Dr. Strangelove* (or *A Clockwork Orange* or *Barry Lyndon*), however, Kubrick can be heard narrating a 17-minute show reel of *Strangelove* excerpts highlighting the principal actors and key scenes for U.S. exhibitors in advance of the film's American release. The demonstration reel appeared online only a few years ago but is of great value since the producer-director-co-writer summarizes the plot and context in his own words and voice (including naturalistic 'ums' and 'ahs'), providing subtle inflection to signify aspects of the satirical humor.[5] For example, over the scene of a bikini clad woman answering a phone call, Kubrick narrates:

> In this scene [Kubrick coughs to clear his throat] we find General 'Buck' Turgidson, the Chairman of the Joint Chiefs of Staff, played by George Scott, and his secretary, Tracy Reed, catching up on some paperwork at three o'clock in the morning in a Washington hotel room.

Unlike *Dr. Strangelove*, there is official film of *2001*—a brief interview with Kubrick at the film's New York premiere in 1968, and behind the scenes footage from a short documentary, *2001: A Space Odyssey: A Look Behind the Future*, promoting this "unusual motion picture" (Thomas Craven n.d.). The latter is introduced by *Look* magazine's publisher, Vernon Myers, and opens on the MGM Studios at Borehamwood and concentrates on the futuristic design, complex space model work, and imagined twenty-first-century technologies. Kubrick is shown sporting a trim beard, seated and relaxed before microphones and a closed circuit TV, outside of the huge, rotating Discovery centrifuge. While Kubrick affably communicates with people inside the set and others (unseen) at his side and over his shoulder the narrator intones: "by remote control Stanley Kubrick directs his actors in complex deep space sequences. He uses concealed television cameras to monitor their performances." The director is shown elsewhere carrying a large boxlike Panavision viewfinder, in genial discussion with the film crew inside the centrifuge set, pausing to line-up various camera angles.

Other behind-the-scenes footage from the same period captures Kubrick wearing a charcoal gray jacket with two pens in his outer breast pocket, filming inside the Discovery pod bay. He moves amiably amongst the crew, liaising with Director of Photography, Geoffrey Unsworth, and sits in his director's chair silently observing set-ups and lighting. These scenes depict Kubrick as an impassive and seemingly imperturbable presence, views of him devoid of giving 'direction' to either cast or crew.

Similar to the *Lolita* newsreel, a Dutch television crew filmed Kubrick attending the New York premiere of *2001* inside Loew's Capitol theater lobby. Wearing a tuxedo and with a short beard, Kubrick is framed in a tight close-up, detailing the "current scientific belief" concerning the possibility of extraterrestrial life in the universe. Christiane and his three daughters can be seen briefly in the background while a second camera records Kubrick's responses from further across the foyer. Despite the crowd and noise his comments are erudite and focused, only hesitating and pausing briefly to shift emphasis away from detailing "the story" towards astronomical and cosmological "facts." After his death, Christiane related that Stanley hated such *vox pop* interviews, where a microphone would be thrust in his face and he had to spontaneously perform. He had "real stage fright [and] couldn't think of a thing to say," she recalled. As much as possible Kubrick avoided such interviews, worried that he would "look like an idiot," not remembering names and dates, while being put "on the spot" (Kubrick 2011). A fear of appearing "foolish" was a major reason why Kubrick consistently refused to appear on chat shows or other broadcast media to discuss his films.

The most widely available behind-the-scenes footage of Kubrick is the documentary made by his daughter Vivian (who was in her late teens at the time), to accompany the 1980 American release of *The Shining*. The portrayal of the filmmaker by Vivian remains the most sustained and unfettered film imagery of Kubrick on screen. It has also provoked controversy concerning the director's treatment of co-star, Shelley Duvall, who claims that he made her life "unbearable" during production (Ebert 1980). Vivian's total access to her father and the production enables a remarkably candid portrayal of the cast and crew.

In his introduction to the 1999 BBC re-screening of Vivian's documentary for the *Arena* program, producer Alan Yentob directly addresses the camera/audience, detailing how Kubrick's vision for the final edit was "to cut out as much of himself as possible," something both Vivian and Yentob objected to, and a position Kubrick ultimately failed to impose despite his vehement protests to daughter and producer. However, as Richard Combs (1996) suggests, what is revelatory about this documentary is Kubrick's *ordinariness*, apparent down to his Bronx accent and unremarkable, though surprisingly youthful, voice.[6]

Kubrick is first seen at the end of a long corridor on the Overlook Hotel set, returning the salute of Jack Nicholson as he approaches, with Vivian filming from behind. Leon Vitali is at Kubrick's side, with the director (bespectacled and bushy bearded) wearing a large green anorak. Throughout the documentary Kubrick is shown undertaking a range of directorial activities, such as using a megaphone while watching a video split to instruct child actor Danny Lloyd (Danny Torrance) to run and hide inside the Overlook's cupboards: "Tell Danny to listen to me Leon. . . . Look back again Danny . . . scared Danny . . . look back Danny . . . start to slow down . . . get in the cupboard . . . fast as you can." The action is intercut with shots used in the film, and followed by Kubrick approaching D.O.P. Douglas Milsome, and happily acknowledging the last three takes "were good."

While in the large Overlook kitchen set Vivian's handheld camerawork captures the routine business of filmmaking, such as Jack Nicholson and Shelley Duvall rehearsing new lines while Kubrick is seen clacking away on a manual typewriter. The banality of the scene is matched by the actors' flat tonal delivery and the director's staccato keystroke percussion. More interesting is when Kubrick is shown inside the Overlook storeroom, trying different camera angles, lying on the floor with a viewfinder, directing Nicholson to look down at the lens while he delivers his lines. Both of these shots depict Kubrick as entirely 'hands-on,' neither precious about doing his own typing nor getting down and dirty on the set to establish camera setups. This is in contrast with a scene where Kubrick is discussing technical aspects of the production with his mother, Gerty, when she visits the set and sits with her filmmaker son while playfully chating with Nicholson about daily changes to the script. Other visitors include *Lolita* star James Mason (in period costume and make up from a different film) and a party of sightseers, with Kubrick and Nicholson smiling and politely welcoming them on set.

Duvall, however, is presented as a self-admitted attention-seeker, complaining of being ill for months and losing her hair from stress. In one sequence, Kubrick tells the crew "Don't sympathize with Shelley" as the actor rolls her eyes dismissively at Vivian's camera in response. Approaching the vast snowbound and foggy hedge maze set, Vivian moves with Kubrick as he barks orders over his shoulder to the crew following him. He seems impatient, yelling: "We're out of time!" Inside the maze Kubrick plays creepy mood music on set and shouts instructions to Danny, while both he and steadicam operator (Garrett Brown) chase Danny through the labyrinth. Notorious for *not* giving direction Kubrick is later shown advising Nicholson and Duvall after a take in the Torrance family bedroom: "Well, many parts of that were good. There were quite a few fuck-ups, but many parts of it were very good." As they wait for video playback Nicholson enquires what was "wrong." Kubrick softens: "I didn't think you got *mean* enough in the beginning [. . .] at the transitional point." He then turns his attention to Duvall:

> The only part *clearly* wrong was at the end when you said 'We've got to get him out of here,' as you got strong at the end, and I think it has to be a last, desperate begging . . . you know.

Vivian frames her father in a tight close-up standing next to a bright table lamp. He looks off camera at the unseen Duvall, adding and waving his clenched left fist for emphasis: "And I *still* think you shouldn't jump on every, single emphatic line. It looks fake. It really does." Duvall disagrees, noting her nervousness, to which Kubrick replies, jerking to mirror her action: "Every time he speaks emphatically, you're jumping and it looks phony." Working on the script together, Duvall seeks to rearrange the sequencing, but Kubrick says: "Honestly, I don't think the lines are gonna make a great deal of difference if you get the right . . . [he pauses slightly to look at her directly] . . . attitude." Kubrick then adds paternally, sotto voce: "I think you're worrying about the wrong thing." A later confrontation with Duvall erupts as Kubrick directs a complex outdoor shot with a large crew involving vast amounts of fog (smoke) and fake snow. Due to technical delays and instruction not being followed tempers flare when Duvall fails to exit the Overlook's massive front doors, on cue. Apparently fuming,

Kubrick marches up to Duvall and berates her tardiness. The (quickly defused) confrontation is later reappraised on camera by the actress as a "game." The "butting of heads together" was needed for the scene to evoke "anger" in Duvall, and the "bollocking" she received helped her concentrate and build up "emotion."

Between *The Shining* and *Full Metal Jacket*, computer consultant Alan Bowker recorded two private encounters with Kubrick on video at Childwickbury in 1983 and 1984.[7] The content is mostly utilitarian and perfunctory. In the first sequence Kubrick and brother-in-law/Executive Producer, Jan Harlan, are shown in an office discussing the potential use of Bowker's "quiet" video camera for shooting location footage. Bowker frames the seated Kubrick from above, in mid-shot, and is heard off-camera, in jest, introducing the video: ". . . with The Stanley Kubrick Story" to which Kubrick instantly fires back, sardonically: "Alex de Large, right?" Bowker zooms in and asks casually: "What would you like for Christmas, Stanley?" Kubrick's demeanor changes to a grin, his head tilted slightly to the left. Staring directly at the camera, he pauses and smiles, offering: "A . . . um . . . Fortune computer." Bowker playfully questions Kubrick further, eliciting more detail from his terse replies about the desired computer's operating software and chip architecture. But Kubrick shifts his posture and looks down, appearing hesitant, somewhat uncomfortable and perhaps even shy. He continues: "I . . ." but catches himself, pausing, and stutters slightly: "L . . . let's play it back." The second video clip is set in a larger workspace where multiple personal computers are on display. While Kubrick asks Bowker about the best sources of information outside of manuals, the computer expert nonchalantly replies "user groups" and records vision of Kubrick's dozing cats, numerous files, office layout, and 'big boards' showing production schedules and other information. It is a testament to Kubrick's trust that he permitted Bowker to record in this manner and did not require him to immediately destroy the video, especially as he had captured production details that Kubrick normally guarded stringently as commercial-in-confidence. Throughout, Kubrick is revealed to be relaxed and inquisitive, tolerant of his felines' repose throughout the office and the questioning from Bowker.

Rarer still are the many hours (18+) of raw material captured by Vivian on location while recording her father during the filming of *Full Metal Jacket*. Snippets from this documentary trove have appeared in related biographical programs such as *LiP* and *Stanley Kubrick's Boxes* (Dir: Jon Ronson 2008). Excerpts can also be seen when visiting the touring Stanley Kubrick Exhibition. Ronson's documentary includes Vivan's footage, often showing Kubrick in a light teal anorak on location at the abandoned Beckton gas works in London, partly demolished for the film production and dressed to look like the Vietnamese city of Hue, circa 1968. Kubrick is seen checking the camera angles on four large 35mm film cameras, running in parallel, and then tersely negotiating the crew's union-mandated 'tea break': "Well we fucked around for an hour and twenty minutes [. . .] If you had a tea break at four you don't have to break for *this* tea break," adding with slight sarcasm: "This must just be a 'complimentary' tea break." All the while Vivian orbits around her seated father, revealing the cast and crew and extras milling about in the foreground and background, waiting: "If you broke for tea at four you don't have to break for tea at six [Kubrick looks at his watch, skeptically], and then break for a meal at seven-thirty. So, figure it out." Throughout the exchange Kubrick's voice is calm and reasoned. Unexpectedly, the interjection of his burley British assistant director, Terry Needham, adds (unnecessary, and likely unwelcome) reinforcement: "I'd prefer to do away with 'em all, 'cos it gives me more fuckin' headaches, poxy tea breaks, than anything else. I'd fucking sling 'em right down that fucking piss hole." Kubrick is bemused by the invective and stands next to his assistant, laughing and looking into Vivian's camera, dismissively: "Right, Terry."

On the set of the Parris Island marine barracks Kubrick is again seen seated, this time instructing his actors to grab their crutches, smirking slightly at the comic movement: "They should *only* do it when they say 'this is my gun,' and then *let go* again, [demonstrating] 'this is for fighting, this is for fun'." The sequence is intercut with behind-the-scenes footage of Douglas Milsome on a camera dolly reversing backwards as marines in underwear run by with raised carbines, reciting "This is my rifle, this is my gun" while thrusting their genitals upward. Standing next to his assistant, Leon Vitali, Kubrick reiterates the motion in front of a throng of actors and extras, grabbing at and jerking his own groin: "There's three beats when you do it. It should be three shakes [laughter]. No, in time to the thing [. . .] So give it three, 'cos a lot of people are still 'touch and go' with what they're doing." The obvious mirth displayed in such scenes, and other film crew pranks involving groups of extras, counter balances the "hard task master" recollections of Kubrick's collaborators during production.

Fictive Kubrick

As a fictionalized character with a distinct screen persona, 'Stanley Kubrick' in feature films only emerged sporadically and mostly after his death. The first film to offer a dramatic realization of the filmmaker was the low-budget U.S. production, *Stranger's Kiss* (1983). Rarely seen today, it was co-written and directed by Matthew Chapman, with the plot oddly reworking Kubrick's second feature, *Killer's Kiss*, rendered as a nostalgic 1980s neo-noir. Aesthetically and dramatically flawed *Stranger's Kiss* remains an ineffectual pastiche when compared to earlier, postmodern remakes/homages from the period, (e.g. *The Postman Always Rings Twice* [1981] and *Body Heat* [1981]).[8] Though bearing little resemblance to the real Kubrick, either visually or verbally, a tall and gangly Peter Coyote plays the fictive director "Stanley," with a nasally tone reminiscent of Henry Fonda. In her *New York Times* review Janet Maslin nevertheless found merit in Coyote's performance, if nothing else:

> Coyote is outstandingly good; he has an assurance bordering on villainy as the Director and brings a shrewd sense of irony to the role. But neither the screenplay nor the performance makes it entirely clear whether the movie he's directing is supposed to be better or worse than the one we are watching.
>
> (Maslin 1984)

While Coyote suggests something of the stereotypical Svengali, a personality trait largely anathema to Kubrick, it is the film's producer "Harris" who is rendered most shabbily. Harris is portrayed as an insipid cypher in the film, a combination of Stanley's gopher and whipping boy.

Playing a support role opposite Geoffrey Rush in *The Life and Death of Peter Sellers*, Stanley Tucci characterizes Kubrick at the time of filming *Dr. Strangelove* cajoling Sellers into performing all four roles to which he has been contractually assigned. Having only the slightest resemblance to the filmmaker, Tucci's 'Kubrick' looks more like a 1950s G-man or private dick, wearing a dark mac overcoat, black boots and wide brimmed hat, and shown sneaking about a hotel corridor.

As one of the film's recurring performative conceits, an almost imperceptible shift briefly depicts Rush playing Kubrick while made up as Tucci.[9] Sitting in the back seat of a moving limousine (which itself is revealed to be a prop using rear projection), a cutaway from Rush as Sellers back to Rush as Tucci (playing Kubrick), provides a curious insight into the filmmaker's on the record observations of the famous character actor, performed by a chameleon-like hybrid of Rush-Sellers-Tucci-Kubrick.

If the scripted and fluid persona of Peter Sellers, as played by the shape-shifting Rush, overlaps with other characters intersecting the actor's life (such as Kubrick or Sellers' mother), it is eclipsed by the bizarre and preposterous real-life impersonations of Kubrick by confidence trickster Allan Conway. Based on "an idiot *pretending* to be" Kubrick (Frewin 2007), Conway—an alcoholic with a lengthy criminal past—wined and dined his way into the confidence of numerous male suitors, from former rent boys to actors and writers. In *Colour Me Kubrick* (Dir: Brian Cook 2006, written by Anthony Frewin) John Malkovich plays Conway as a tragic and shameless conman who bluffs his way around the U.K. and Europe pretending to be the famous filmmaker. Malkovich's performance (Conway-as-Kubrick) is both hilarious and poignant in its destructive invocation of hedonism and ennui. As with Coyote before him, Malkovich's campy Conway is self-consciously light-years away from either Kubrick's physique or verbal timbre. As preposterous at it seems, the film authentically documents many of the scams that Conway perpetrated, defrauding individuals out of large and petty sums, while mostly avoiding public exposure or recourse. In one memorable scene, a hospitalized Conway tells nursing staff: "I'm Stanley Kubrick," as fellow inmates (black and elderly) parrot in defiance, à la *Spartacus*, "I'm Stanley Kubrick!"

Kubrick as an imagined character is also manifest in recent feature dramas, such Robert Sheenhan's portrayal in *Moonwalkers* (Dir: Antoine Bardou-Jacquet 2015) as a bearded hippy, improbably dragooned into impersonating Kubrick in order to fleece the C.I.A. out of secret funds for faking the Apollo moon landing footage. Although replete with numerous and sometimes inventive nods to Kubrick's oeuvre, the film remains a desultory post-millennial comedy. Riffing off the same mythology is *Operation Avalanche* (Dir: Matt Johnson 2015) which chiefly obscures any overt influence of Kubrick by representing him as an unseen but ever-present artistic force, overshadowing this mostly lame conspiracy caper's plot.

Irrespective of the individual agendas of these feature films and their varying degree of Kubrick character integrity, curiously none of them play to the common (mis)conceptions of the filmmaker as a recluse, or impeded by common phobias (e.g. aviophobia or tachophobia). Perhaps with Kubrick's passing at the turn of the millennium the previous media opprobrium and character assassination was no longer justifiable or sustainable.

As performer

Regarded as a shy, awkward kid from the Bronx, Kubrick remained an avid filmgoer throughout his early childhood, often cutting school to see double features at local cinemas. While working at *Look* magazine Kubrick would try to watch every movie shown in New York during the late 1940s to early 1950s. In preparation for his initial forays into filmmaking he began reading Pudovkin for film technique and Stanislavsky on working with actors. However, before embarking on his independent, self-taught motion picture work in the early 1950s, the young Stanley Kubrick appears, unremarkably, as an extra in the seminal experimental feature *Dreams That Money Can Buy* (1947), developed, produced, and directed by Hans Richter (1943–1947).[10]

I am deeply grateful to author Anthony Frewin, Kubrick's long-time assistant, for alerting me to his discovery of this previously unknown Kubrick screen appearance.[11]

Richter's color fantasy film presents an anthology of collaborative sequences by leading twentieth-century artists comprising: Max Ernst, Man Ray, Marcel Duchamp, Fernand Leger, and Alexander Calder, with scores by avant-garde musicians such as John Cage and Darius Milhaud. Shot on location in and around New York, and part-funded by Peggy Guggenheim, the film self-consciously foregrounds "psychology" in seven interwoven dream sequences (Northwest Film Forum 2014). Although the appearance of the 19-year-old Stanley Kubrick is quite brief (and literally alongside his soon-to-be wife, Toba Metz) the image of the teenage photographer in this context is both surprising and revelatory; surprising in that, to date, it has escaped the scrutiny of researchers and biographers, and revelatory for the range of potential influences it had on Kubrick's later life and work. For example, just as his early cineaste exposure to screen sequences have had demonstrable influence on the filmmaker (e.g. the patriarchal ax attack in *The Phantom Carriage* [1921]), in Dream 2: *The Girl with the Prefabricated Heart*, naked and dismembered store dummies are presented in a manner that pre-figures the surreal setting of the final fight sequence in *Killer's Kiss* amid warehouse mannequins.

Dream 3: *Ruth, Roses and Revolvers*, which briefly captures Kubrick and Metz, also features Kubrick's future second-wife, Ruth Sobotka, as the eponymous title character and co-lead actor. Conceived and written by Man Ray, *Ruth, Roses and Revolvers* was realized by Richter who is credited as director, producer, and designer. The sequence depicts a well-dressed young couple (Sobotka and Arthur Seymour) attending a film screening in a suburban basement theater. Kubrick and Metz are among the audience, shown seated in the second row of wooden chairs. Intercut between a glamorous hostess (Evelyn Hausman), who stands before the screen and introduces the movie, we see Kubrick in his first cutaway, center-framed and in mid-background, wearing a pale brown jacket and lightly tinted glasses. The second cutaway is shot over the hostess' shoulders with Kubrick again framed in the middle, this time without spectacles, applauding alongside others, and then reaching inside his jacket pocket. Metz is seen at his side, screen left.[12] The final shot that recognizably shows Kubrick (though not Metz) has him framed in the foreground at bottom left, imitating the action (along with most other extras in the audience) of an unnamed character on screen; actually, scenarist Man Ray in an uncredited role. While Kubrick's participation and performance as an anonymous extra is unremarkable and unexceptional, it undoubtedly gave Kubrick insight into direction and acting, and an early introduction to contemporary, independent low-budget filmmaking outside of the studio system.

Although filmed some months before Kubrick would move into a Greenwich Village apartment with Metz, the *Look* staff photographer was meeting his fair share of American and international artists, actors, and celebrities while on assignment at home and abroad. By late 1948 Kubrick was also determined to advance beyond his stills work, telling a journalist that he was "very serious about cinematography, and [. . .] about to start filming a sound production written and financed by himself and several friends" (Stagg 1948). This article ran a full 18 months before Kubrick began work on his debut film, the short 35mm newsreel *Day of the Fight* (released in 1951).

Bookending a half-century screen career, Kubrick's only other known performance to camera was his 1997 acceptance speech for the Director's Guild of America D.W. Griffith Lifetime Achievement Award. The prestigious honor was bestowed in absentia while Kubrick was in production on *Eyes Wide Shut*. Regardless, it is almost certain the filmmaker would never have returned to North America to accept it in person.

The pre-recorded video portrays Kubrick in medium close-up wearing a dark jacket, button-down blue shirt, and no tie. His receding hair is mostly dark and styled naturally, his gray beard bushy, giving him an overall rabbinical air. Kubrick stares straight into the camera and delivers his three-minute speech in a single take. Though baggy lidded, his eyes are keen with his dark pupils partly obscured by circular, wire-framed glasses. Perhaps due to the single source key lighting there is no sign of Kubrick's signature dark-rimmed sockets. While his poise is obviously considered and composed, the effect is mostly "stiff" (Swanky 2013). As his wife Christiane recalled, laughing and shaking her head at the memory, he looked "as if he'd swallowed a broom stick . . . all rigid . . . and he would kill his own jokes [. . .] he was terrified" (Kubrick 2011). Self-directed by Kubrick, when watching the playback both Christiane and his assistant Leon Vitali cheekily "mocked" the auteur as he redid take-after-take until he finally decided that he was out of time and sent it off. When Kubrick saw it televised, Christiane relates that he was mortified at his performance, and he buried his head in his arms.

However, on screen, Kubrick's tone is measured and his delivery controlled. He apologizes for not being present at the ceremony, noting that at the time of the DGA award presentation "I'm probably in my car on the way to the studio." The filmmaker shifts ever so slightly from right-to-left, hinting at his discomfort, and raises his right hand to adjust his spectacles, perhaps to improve his view of the off-screen text he is reading (Kubrick 2011).

Yet it is perhaps a mark of Kubrick's humility that his brief monologue foregrounds what he calls a "profound" observation by his friend, Stephen Spielberg, when describing the "most difficult and challenging thing about directing a film." Similarly, Kubrick uses most of the remainder of his speech to honor the accomplishments and the spectacular rise and fall of Griffith, as a "cautionary tale," but then injects his own inimitable sense of irony and wry humor. In an inventive and novel stratagem he offers a unique artistic perspective on Griffith, comparing the silent era film pioneer to the "myth of Icarus." With the virtuoso gambit of a chess grand master he undermines the fable's traditional precept about hubris—rather than moralizing "don't try to fly too high," instead: "forget the wax and feathers and do a better job on the wings"—to subvert both conventional wisdom and film industry practice, something for which Kubrick was himself renown.

Currently, with no available behind-the-scenes video of Kubrick on screen directing *Eyes Wide Shut*, the DGA acceptance video remains his autobiographical swan song. It is fitting then, while "humbly" thanking the DGA for the award, Kubrick concludes his declamation by praising Griffith's monumental achievements, noting that, irrespective of Griffith's preceding history, "one thing is certain, he left us with an inspiring and intriguing legacy."

In retrospect this resolute pronouncement and denouement might be equally considered Kubrick's own, understated and self-conscious, epitaph.

Notes

1 Prior to this Kubrick gave a brief radio interview to CBS in December 1958 (www.archiviokubrick.it/english/words/interviews/1958cbsradio.html). In 1982 Hitchcock authority Ken Mogg gave me a copy of a recorded interview with Kubrick (circa 1972) conducted by an unnamed Australia journalist after the release of *A Clockwork Orange*. Apart from the appalling baiting by the inane reporter repeating the clichés about Kubrick being a non-flying, hard-hat wearing, slow-driving recluse, it struck me how *youthful* and warm (and tolerant!) Kubrick's voice was during this encounter.
2 Kubrick refused to allow a *Newsweek* staff photographer to take the cover photo, arguing with the editor (and winning), supplying a range of images he composed and shot of himself.
3 A year or so later Kubrick chanced upon an intruder in the gardens of his Abbots Mead home but not long after left the U.K. to film *Barry Lyndon* in Ireland.
4 There are multiple stories about I.R.A. threats, including "an agent of Britain's Special Branch, which monitors national security, called his production office at Ardmore, in County Waterford, to warn Kubrick that their intelligence determined he was a potential target of the IRA" (Ghosh 2013). See also: Maria Pramaggiore, *Making Time in Stanley Kubrick's Barry Lyndon: Art, History, and Empire* (London: Bloomsbury, 2014).

5 Kubrick also recorded himself for *2001* (as sound effects for the astronauts, by respiring and breathing heavily inside a space helmet). He is also rumored to have uncredited voiceovers in *The Shining* and *Full Metal Jacket*.
6 To this day fans still encountering Kubrick's voice for the first-time offer comments online such as [sic]: "i actually get to hear the genius talk :O"; "It's so funny hearing his Bronx accent and even he's a real big guy he doesn't have a real deep voice. It's so shocking and weird! Hahahaha it's so funny!"; "to think ive never heard his voice before today"; "Oh man, I love his voice!"; "I expectet him to have a deeper voice"; "Seems Kubrick's accent is part British, part staunch New Yorker."
7 Kubrick seems to wear the exact same clothes in both clips—a gray zip-up jacket, blue tee shirt, and dark trousers. This may be a coincidence, suggest his limited range of clothing, or mean the clips were actually taken at the same time. It may just be the range, as Tony Frewin related by email Kubrick said to him about buying multiple copies of new clothes: "It means you don't have to go out again shopping, and you don't waste time having to decide what to wear" (Frewin August 22, 2018).
8 As Anthony Frewin noted by email, Kubrick never saw the film: "I doubt SK would have gone more than ten minutes in to this movie. He would have given it to me for a report!" (Frewin December 22, 2017).
9 Oddly, in this guise Rush looks more like Gabriel Byrne, rather than either Tucci or Kubrick.
10 Richter was a professor at City College of New York during the 1940s when Kubrick attended night school. The film production was promoted widely, with Richter noting later that it received so much free publicity that he was swamped with offers from volunteers and pro-bono help.
11 Anthony Frewin related the find: "I only realized this after he had passed. He never mentioned it to me" (Frewin 2017).
12 The montage suggests that the preceding shot of Kubrick with glasses has been edited out of linear order since he is not returning his glasses to his pocket but the reverse. Presumably this was an action taken under the direction of Richter, since no other character is shown so clearly wearing glasses, and Kubrick at that point in life was not bespectacled. Hence, the glasses are likely a prop that Kubrick dons, acting as an extra under direction from filmmaker Richter.

Works cited

Barter, Pavel. 2013. *Castles, Candles and Kubrick*. October 19. www.youtube.com/watch?v=6mGyaF1N3pA.

Benson, Michael. 2018. *Space Odyssey: Stanley Kubrick, Arthur C. Clarke, and the Making of a Masterpiece*. New York: Simon & Schuster.

Brosnahan, Cori. 2017. "Personalizing the Past: History Through Home Movies." August 9. www.pbs.org/wgbh/americanexperience/features/personalizing-past-interview-rick-prelinger/.

Combs, Richard. 1996. "Kubrick Talks!" *Film Comment*, 32, September/October: 81.

Ebert, Roger. 1980. "Interview with Shelley Duvall." December 14. www.rogerebert.com/interviews/interview-with-shelley-duvall.

Frewin, Anthony. 2007. "Color Him Kubrick!" *StopSmiling*, no. 23, March 30. www.stopsmilingonline.com/story_detail.php?id=777.

———. 2017. Email correspondence, December 15.

Ghosh, Palash. 2013. "Stanley Kubrick's Irish Odyssey: Why the IRA Forced the Director Off the Emerald Isle During Filming of 'Barry Lyndon.'" *International Business Times*, November 13. www.ibtimes.com/stanley-kubricks-irish-odyssey-why-ira-forced-director-emerald-isle-during-filming-barry-lyndon.

Kubrick, Christiane. 2011. "Stanley Was not a Good Actor." *The Stanley & Us Project*. https://vimeo.com/channels/stanleyandus/28271569.

Kubrick, Katharina. 2012. "Katharina Kubrick, 'Crazy Time.'" *The Stanley & Us Project*. www.youtube.com/watch?v=-8NAabbBpes.

———. 2014. *Kubrick Remembered*. Directed by Gary Khammar. Warner Brothers Entertainment.

Maslin, Janet. 1984. "'Stranger's Kiss,' in the Hollywood of 1955." *The New York Times*, August 13. www.nytimes.com/1984/08/13/movies/strangers-kiss-in-the-hollywood-of-1955.html.

Northwest Film Forum. 2014. *Dreams that Money Can Buy*. Program Notes. Seattle, WA: The Sprocket Society.

Simpson, Garry E. 2008. "Whose Stanley Kubrick? The Myth, Legacy and Ownership of the Kubrick Image." In *Stanley Kubrick: Essays on His Films and Legacy*, edited by Gary D. Rhodes, 232–44. Jefferson, NC: McFarland.

Stagg, Mildred. 1948. "Camera Quiz Kid: Stan Kubrick." *The Camera*. October. www.archiviokubrick.it/english/words/interviews/1948cameraquiz.html#

Swanky, Shawn. 2013. "How Stanley Kubrick Felt About His D.W. Griffith A ward Speech." March 8. www.shawnswanky.com/shawns-picks/christiane-kubrick-on-stanleys-griffith-award-speech/.

Thomas Craven Film Corporation. n.d. *2001: A Space Odyssey: A Look Behind the Future*. New York. www.youtube.com/watch?v=eeGI1FoySaE.

Zimmerman, Patricia. 2008. "The Home Movie Moment: Excavations, Moments, Minings." In *Mining the Home Movie: Excavations in Histories and Memories*, edited by Karen L. Ishizuka and Patricia Rodden Zimmermann, 1–28. Berkeley, CA: California University Press.

Conclusion

Mick Broderick

In some small way *The Kubrick Legacy* has sought to contribute to the existing scholarship that attests to the tangible cultural resonances of Stanley Kubrick's life and work. While there is much to admire in Kubrick's astonishing oeuvre and proclivity for virtuoso display, he had (and continues to have) his trenchant critics and detractors. Perhaps this is rightfully so, since Kubrick never appeared to play it safe. A polymathic artist and polemicist of his stature endeavoring to produce commercially successful films for the international mass entertainment market, creating risk-taking works intended to remain relevant for generations, *should* elicit controversy and, therefore, logically endure condemnation from some quarters.

Kubrick's profound and singular vision resolutely returned to explore many defining aspects of 'the human condition'—whether that be found in 4 million year-old proto-human man-apes; pre-Christian slaves and the empires of antiquity; the mores of Enlightenment Europe; the relentless militarism of the twentieth century embracing total war, genocide, and nuclear Armageddon; the complexity of contemporary fears and sexual desires; or post-human supermen, extraterrestrials, and artificial intelligences—hence his lasting appeal as a major creative intellect and artist.

Apart from those recent influences identified in this book's Introduction, further recognition of the filmmaker's legacy is apparent in the performance of the director's script for the abandoned *Napoleon* project (1969–1973) by New York's Angel Orensanz Foundation. This Off-Broadway "world premiere, staged reading," adapted by and starring David Serero, complements previous events such as the popular iterations of *Dr. Strangelove* live readings (Chicago, Boston, and Los Angeles). Meanwhile, Malcolm McDowell hosted *Stanley Kubrick's Sound Odyssey*, a series of concerts performing Stanley Kubrick film scores at the Walt Disney Concert Hall (Worthington 2018).

Conclusion

The *2001* re-release continued to push exhibition boundaries with an additional IMAX 4k laser series of limited digital screenings at 350 venues world-wide. Just as this landmark film remains topical and relevant, so too does Kubrick fandom that spans generations. On the anniversary date of the filmmaker's birthday *Mad Magazine* published a social media meme, reprinting its June 1973 "Crockwork Lemon" cover, under the heading:

> Orange you glad it's a special droog's 90th Birthday?
> Mad salute Stanley Kubrick!

Another recent development in Kubrick fandom is the semi-regular, episodic production of *Kubrick's Universe: The Stanley Kubrick Podcast* by Jason Furlong, Stephen Rigg, Mark Lentz, and James Marinaccio of the Stanley Kubrick Appreciation Society, featuring interviews with Kubrick collaborators, cast and crew, academics, and fans (Kubrick's Universe 2018). Similarly, *The Kubrick Series* podcast was granted special permission to release Tim Cahill's two-hour raw interview tape with Kubrick from his 1987 *Rolling Stone* interview (KubrickU 2018).

Kubrick's twice-abandoned *Napoleon* project is now slated for production as a much anticipated mini-series for HBO, adapted by David Leland and with Cary Fukunaga named as a possible director (Holdsworth 2016). The rediscovery by Nathan Abrams of *Burning Secret*—Kubrick's unproduced screenplay, co-authored with Calder Willingham adapting Stefan Zweig's 1913 novella shortly before he worked again with Willingham on *Paths of Glory* (1957)—unleashed a flurry of interest by producers ahead of its auction by Bonhams in New York, selling for US$38,000 (Sharf 2018).

Anticipating the decade ahead—between the 20th anniversary of the director's death (March 2019) and the centenary of his birth (July 2028)—there will be multiple opportunities for commemorative events (i.e. the 20th anniversary of *Eyes Wide Shut* in 2019 and the 50th anniversaries of *A Clockwork Orange* in 2022 and *Barry Lyndon* in 2025) alongside live performances, retrospectives, exhibitions, testimonials, revelations, and reinterpretations.

One thing seems certain: for some time to come Kubrick will continue to grow in stature as a giant amongst his twentieth-century filmmaking contemporaries, dwarfing his many acolytes, imitators, and wannabes past, present, and future.

Works cited

Holdsworth, Nick. 2016. "Cary Fukunaga in Talks to Direct HBO Stanley Kubrick Mini 'Napoleon,' From Steven Spielberg." *Hollywood Reporter*, May 20. www.hollywoodreporter.com/live-feed/cary-fukunaga-talks-direct-hbo-895532.

KubrickU. 2018. "Amazing Unearthed 1987 Audio Interview W/Kubrick by Tim Cahill!" May 12. KubrickU.blogspot.com.

Sharf, Zac. 2018. "Stanley Kubrick's Lost Script 'Burning Secret' Set for Auction, Draws 'Lolita' and 'Eyes Wide Shut' Comparisons." November 7. www.indiewire.com/2018/11/stanley-kubrick-burning-secret-lost-script-auction-1202018779/.

Worthington, Clint. 2018. "Malcolm McDowell Hosting a Concert Series of Stanley Kubrick Film Scores." November 6. https://consequenceofsound.net/2018/11/malcolm-mcdowell-stanley-kubrick-music-series/.

Index

Abbotts Mead 92
Abrams, N. 2, 59, 107
Academy Awards 13, 47; advertisements 74
Adams, M. 2
Addams Family 89
Adelaide Symphony Orchestra 72
advertising (including commercials) 4; the Kubrick oeuvre 79–80; music in 81; unintended legacy 80–81; *see also* individual films
Age of Innocence, The (1993) 47
A.I.: Artificial Intelligence (2000) 19n7
Also Sprach Zarathustra 41, 44, 71, 74, 77
ambiguity 52, 54, 63, 64
American Cinematographer 88
Anderson, W. 48
apocalypticism 23
Archive of American Television 39
Arena (BBC) 95
Aristotle 55–56
Aryan Papers 19n7, 59
Ascher, R. 4, 53

B-52 41
"Baby Did a Bad Thing" 79
Bach, J.S. 47, 49
Balzer, D. 10
Bardou-Jacquet, A. 100
Barry Lyndon (1975) 2, 13, 37, 107; in advertising 77; music in 42, 46
Barthes, R. 62–63
Bartók, B. 42
Bass, S. 14

Baxter, J. 16
Beckton gas works 97
Beethoven, L. van 42, 48, 77
behind-the-scenes 5, 94–98
Benjamin, W. 16
Benson, M. 1,
Bernstein, J. 5n2
Bertolucci, B. 48
Bing 74
Birch, S. (*The Barmecide Feast*) 1
Birth of a Nation (1915) 38, 46
Blackboard Jungle, The (1955) 39
Blakemore, B. 55, 59
"Blue Danube" 79
Body Heat (1981) 99
bomb (atomic, nuclear) *see* nuclear weapons, Doomsday Machine
Bonhams (auctioneers) 3, 107
Bordwell, D. 53, 56, 63
Boulting Brothers 3
Bowker, A. 97
Bowly, A. 72
Bowman, Dave (*2001*) 1, 72
box office 14
British Pathé 93
Britten, B. 48
Broderick, M. 23
Bronx 90, 95, 100
Brown, G. 96
Buren, D. 9
Burning Secret 107
Byrnes, P. 44

Cage, J. 48, 101
Cahill, T. 63, 67, 107

110 Index

Calder, A. 101
Cannes Film Festival 1
Carlos, W. 42
Carlsberg beer 75
Carnival of the Animals 48
Cartoon Network (US) 73
Casino (1995) 47
Castle, P. 76, 82n13
Cavalleria Rusticana 47
censorship 14, 61
Channel Four (UK) 80
Chapman, M. 98
Charlier, P. 44
Chess Life 88
Childwickbury 92
Christmas 78
C.I.A. 100
Ciment, M. 19n10, 46, 61
cinemania 60–61
cinematic language 54
Citizen Kane 15
City College of New York 104n10
Clarke, A.C. 1, 29, 80–81, 83n15, 88
classical music (including art music) 2, 37–38; in advertising 70–74, 76–79
Clemson, G. 19n1
Clockwork Orange, A (1971) 12, 13, 15, 37, 89, 107; in advertising 68–69, 76–77; music in 42; *see also* "Crockwork Lemon"
CNN 73
Cocks, G. 55, 58–59
Coen brothers 48
Color Me Kubrick (2005) 5, 88, 99–100
Columbia Pictures 14
Combs, R. 95
Commander-1 4, 22
commercials *see* advertising; individual films
conspiracies 4, 5, 52, 57, 100
Conway, A. 5, 99–100
Cook, B. 99
Coors beer 76
Coyote, P. 5, 99
Craven, T. 94
Creativity Magazine 82n11
"Crockwork Lemon" 107
Cronkite, W. 24
cues 41–42, 49; musical cue sheet 38

curation 9–10; as collector 17; curator-as-auteur 12
Curtis, T. 75

D'Alessandro, E. 2
Dark Side of the Moon: Stanley Kubrick and the Fake Moon Landings (2014) 4, 52, 60
Daniels, R. 2, 19n1, 24
"Dawn of Man" 70, 71, 81
Day of the Fight (1951) 39, 102
Days of Heaven (1978) 48
Departed, The (2006) 47
Desplat, A. 49
Detroit Free Press, The 88
Deutsches Filmmuseum 1, 8
Dewar's whiskey 72
Dies Irae 42
Director's Guild of America 102
Django Unchained (2012) 47
Donizetti, G. 47
Doomsday Machine 24, 26
dossier (post-Kubrick) 3
Douglas, K. 75, 92, 93
Dreams That Money Can Buy (1947) 100–102
droog 107
Dr. Strangelove (character of) 23
Dr. Strangelove or: How I Learned to Stop Worrying and Love the Bomb (1964) 3, 4, 14, 22, 92; in advertising 68, 75; music in 41; exhibitors' show reel 93
Duchamp, M. 101
Duvall, S. 95–97
D.W. Griffith Lifetime Achievement Award 102

Easy Rider (1969) 39
eBay 2–3
Eco, U. 53–55, 62
Ebert, R. 44
Edison Film Company 38
Eigen, E. 42
Elinor, C. 46
Emerson, J. 52
Encyclopedia of Music for Pictures 38
Epaminondas, A. 2
episteme 56
Ermey, R. Lee 76

Ernst, M. 101
exhibitions 1–3, 7–13; chronological approach 11–12
Eyes Wide Shut (1999) 3, 5, 11, 15, 70, 90, 102, 103, 107; in advertising 70, 78–79, 81; music in 42, 43, 46
"Eyes Wide Shut party" 78

fandom 2, 3, 12, 45, 88, 104n6, 107; Kubrick as fan 67
fascism 22, 27, 28, 30, 32, 34; as Nazism 28, 58–59
Faust 47
Fear and Desire (1953) 11, 13, 19n4; music in 39
Feldman, M. 48
Fenwick, J. 1, 12
Ferro, P. 68–69, 75
Filmworker 2
Fitzmaurice, M. 93
Flying Padre, The (1951) 39
Fonda, H. 99
Fonda, P. 14
Frewin, A. 2, 100, 101, 104n7–8, 104n11
Fried, G. 39, 40
Fugue in D minor 49
Fukunaga, C. 107
Full Metal Jacket (1987) 5, 39, 62, 97, 104n5; in advertising 76, 78; music in 42, 46;Vivian's documentary 97–98
Furlong, J. 107

Gatorade 71
Gaut, B. 55
George, D. 35n18
George, P. 4, 22, 35n9–10, 12–14, 16–18
Geraghty, Commander James William 30
Gesamtkunstwerk 15–16, 17
Ghamari-Tabrizi, S. 23
The Girl with the Prefabricated Heart 101
Goldberg, M. 61
Golden Globe 47
Golden Lion 13
Gold Room 72, 79
Goldsmith, J. 43

"Got Milk?" 73
Gounod, C. 47
Grady girls (*The Shining* twins) 73–74, 81
Gray, J. 9
Greenbaum, N. 71
Greenwich Village 102
Griffith, D.W. 37, 38, 46, 103
Guggenheim, P. 101
guinea pigs 30, 33

HAL 71
Handel, G.F. 41, 42, 77
Hanks, L.H. 11
Harlan, J. 88, 91, 97
Harris, B. 41
Harris, J. B. 40, 90
Hartman, Sgt. (*Full Metal Jacket*) 76
Hateful Eight, The (2015) 47
Hausman, E. 101
HBO 71
Hellbenders, The (1967, aka *The Cruel Ones*) 47
Henry, L. 73
Herrmann, B. 40
Hitchcock, A. 40
Hitler, A. 25
Holocaust 58–59
Holst, G. 45
homage 5, 18, 69, 73–75, 78, 82
Hopkins, A. 79
human zoo 5n1
Hunter, I. Q. 53, 64
Hyundai 71

Ikea 74–75
imitation 45, 67, 69, 78
Infascelli, A. 2
Isaak, C. 79
Italian Romantic opera 47
IMAX 107
intentionalism 58, 62
interpretation 1, 8, 9, 16, 17, 52, 107; in advertising 77
intertextuality 52
I.R.A. 89, 103n4
"It's All Forgotten Now" 42
"I Want a Boy for Christmas" 42
"I Want to Marry a Lighthouse Keeper" 42

112 Index

Jailhouse Rock (1957) 39
James, L. 71
Jaws (1975) 46
jazz 40
"Jazz Suite" 78
Johnson, L. 41, 43
Johnson, M. 100

Kahn, H. 4, 23
Kant, I. 53, 56
Karel, W. 52
Kearns, J. 55
Kia 71
Killer's Kiss (1955) 13, 19n9, 98, 101; music in 39, 40
Killing, The (1956) 13, 19n9; music in 39
Kim, J. 10
King, S. 73
Knight of Cups (2015) 48
Kolker, R. 37
Korngold, E.W. 46
Korova Milkbar 12, 69
Krämer, P. 2, 23, 29, 34n1, 82n1
Kubrick, A. 90–91
Kubrick aides 2, *see also* Frewin, A.; Vitali, L.
Kubrick, B. 89–90
Kubrick By Candlelight (2017) 77
Kubrick, C. 90, 91, 92, 94, 102
Kubrick Cocktail 18, 19n11
Kubrick: The Definitive Edition 19n10
Kubrick estate 11, 74
Kubrick, G. 90, 96
"Kubrickian" 5, 16, 48, 80, 82; *Oxford English Dictionary* 18, 19n12; sensibility 48; space 15
Kubrick, J. 89
Kubrick, K. 91
Kubrick's Odyssey: Secrets Hidden in the Films of Stanley Kubrick; Part One: Kubrick and Apollo 55
Kubrick, S.: acting/performing 98, 101–103; animal lover 92, 97; anniversaries 107; anonymity 88; annotations 17; on chess 12, 16, 88; as collector 16–18; computers 97; continuity errors 16; in documentaries/newsreels 88, 92, 95–97; "hands-on" 95; home movies 89–90, 97; identifiable face 88; impersonator 99–100; interviews with 3, 53–54, 59, 61, 62, 63, 76; Kubrickian space 15; Kubrick-inspired products 69; letters 3, 17; music 15, 37, 106; myths about 17, 89, 92; on-screen character 88, 98–100; polymath 106; his "rosebud" 13; his voice 88, 91, 93, 95, 97, 104n5–6; vox pop 94
Kubrick Series, The (podcast) 107
Kubrick's 2001: 50 Years A Space Odyssey 1
Kubrick's Universe: The Stanley Kubrick Podcast 107
Kubrick, V. 42, 91, 96, 98

LA County Museum of Art (LACMA) 11
LaMotta, J. 47
Last Waltz, The (1978) 48
Leger, F. 101
Legion of Decency 14
Leland, D. 107
Lentz, M. 107
Levi jeans 77
Lexus GS 78–79
Life and Death of Peter Sellers, The (2004) 5, 88, 99
Lifestyles condoms 75
Ligeti, G. 42, 48, 71
live performances 2
Ljujic, T. 2
Lloyd, D. 95
LoBrutto, V. 7, 13, 40, 68
Loew's Capitol theater 94
Lolita (1962) 5, 14, 15, 18, 90, 96; in advertising 76, 81; music in 40–41, 43; newsreel 93, 94
Lolita (character in film) 41
"Lolita Ya-Ya" 41, 76
Lontano 48
Look magazine 19n7, 88, 90, 94, 100
Lovisato, M. 53, 60, 64
Lucas, G. 45–46
Lucia di Lammermoor 47
"Lux Aeterna" 71
Lynn, V. 41
Lyon, S. (*Lolita*) 41, 76

MacMillan, L. 10–11, 12
Mad Magazine 107
Making 'The Shining' (1980) 88
Malick, T. 4, 48–49
Malkovich, J. 100
Maness, F. 92
Mann, A. 40
Man Who Wasn't There, The (2001) 48
Marinaccio, J. 107
Mascagni, P. 47
masked ball 42, 78
masks 3, 30
Maslin, J. 99
Mason, J. 96
Maynard, P. 58
McAvoy, C. 53, 63
McDonald's McCafe 74
McDowell, M. (*A Clockwork Orange*) 106
Mead, A.: *see* Kubrick, V.
Mee, L. 53, 64
memorabilia 2–3, 68
merchandizing 18–19
Metz, T. 101–102
MGM Studios Borehamwood 94
Michelob beer 67
Midnight Cowboy (1969) 39
"Midnight, the Stars, and You" 42, 72
Milhaud, D. 101
Milsome, D. 95, 98
Mogg, K. 103n1
monolith 11, 42, 62; in advertising 69, 70, 71, 81, 82n11
Monthly Film Bulletin 88
Moog synthesizer 42
Moonrise Kingdom (2012) 48
Moonwalkers (2015) 5, 100
Moreira, D. 44
Morricone, E. 47, 48, 49
Motion Picture Moods for Pianists and Organists 38
Museum of the City of New York 2
music 4, 37; musical anachronism 42; pre-existing 40–47; scores 39–50; "temp tracks" 49; *see also* Kubrick, S.; individual film titles
Myers, V. 94
myth of Icarus 103

Napoleon 17, 19n7, 106, 107
NASA 60
Needham, T. 98
neo-formalism 56
New World, The (2005) 48
New York Philharmonic 44
New York Stories (1989) 47
newsreels 5, 92–94
Newsweek 88, 103n3
Nicholson, J. (*The Shining*) 47, 95–96
Nightingale, N. (*Eyes Wide Shut*) 78
nightmare comedy 22, 29, 33, 34
"Ninth Symphony" 77
Noble, R. 72
Nolan, C. 1
North, A. 39, 43, 44, 46
nuclear war 4, 25–28, 29, 30, 32, 34, 106
nuclear weapons 26, 28, 29, 33, 35n14

Obrist, H.U. 15, 16–17
"Once" (Norman Gimbel and Arden Clar) 40
O'Neill, P. 9
one-point perspective 75, 82n12
On Thermonuclear War 23–26
ontology 55
Operation Avalanche (2016) 5, 100
Oportos Fantastic Film Festival 75
Orange 77
Overlook Hotel 18, 59, 60, 72, 74, 75, 95, 96
"Overture to the Sun" 42

parody 45, 79–81, 107
Parris Island 98
Paths of Glory (1957) 107; music in 39, 40
Penderecki, K. 42, 48
Pepsi 71, 75
Perkins, Anthony 67
Phantom Carriage, The (1921)
Philadelphia Orchestra 44
photographs ("Mickey, the Shoeshine Boy") 3
phronesis 64
Pickens, S. (*Dr. Strangelove*) 75
Planets, The 45
Planet of the Apes 71
Plato 55–56

114 *Index*

Playboy 88
Polan, D. 7–8
Pook, J. 42–43, 78
pop score 39, 41
popular culture 4, 53; in music 42, 49
Popular Mechanics 72
post-Kubrick 3
The Postman Always Rings Twice (1981) 99
P.O.V. 80
Powerade 75
Power Tee 71
Premier Inn 73
President Muffley (*Dr. Strangelove*) 25, 31
Presley, E. 39
Princess Margaret 92–93
Puccini, G. 47
Punch 92

Quest, R. 73

Radio Times 72
Raging Bull (1980) 47
Rapée, E. 38
Ray, Man 101
Red Alert 23, 30
Reichmann, H.-P. 8
Richter, H. 100
Riddle, N. 40, 41, 43, 76
Rigg, S. 107
"Rise of Doctor Strangelove, The" 24, 29
Rocket Mortgage 70
"Rocky Mountains" 42
Rolling Stone 67, 69, 107
Ronson, J. 97
room 237 73
Room 237 (2012) 4, 16, 52
Rosenman, L. 41
Rossini, G. 89
Ross, A. 46
Rush, G. 5, 99
Ruth, Roses and Revolvers 101
Ryan, J.F. 55, 60

Saint-Saëns, C. 48
Sante, L. 2
"Sarabande" 41, 77
The Saturday Review 88
Schindler's List (1993) 59

Schnitzler, A. 78
Sci-Fi Channel (U.S.) 73
Scorsese, M. 37, 47–48, 50
Sellers, P. (*Dr. Strangelove*) 5, 25, 31, 88, 90, 99
Serbian Film Festival Kustendorf 72
Serero, D. 106
Seymour, A. 101
Shining, The (1980) 3, 4, 12–19, 37, 52–60, 63, 88, 95, 97, 104n5; in advertising 70, 72–75, 79, 80; music in 37, 39, 42, 43, 46, 48
"Shining/Heartbeat" 42
Shostakovich, D. 70, 78
Shutter Island (2010) 47
Siegelaub, S. 9, 15
Silo Theater 77
Simpson, R.J.E. 18
Simpsons, The 18
S is for Stanley (2015) 2
Sitges Film Festival 79
SkyTV (U.K.) 79
Smirnoff vodka 72
Sobotka, R. 101
"social treasury" (Eco) 55, 62
Sotheby's (auctioneers) 3, 5n2
Southern, T. 92
Spartacus (1960) 13–14, 15, 100; in advertising 69, 75; music in 39; newsreel/premiere 92–93
Spielberg, S. 46, 59, 103
"Spirit in the Sky" 71
Stanley Kubrick Archive (SKA) 2, 7–8, 24, 35n10, 59
Stanley Kubrick: A Biography 7
Stanley Kubrick's Boxes (2008) 5, 97
Stanley Kubrick's A Clockwork Orange: Based on the Novel by Anthony Burgess 3
Stanley Kubrick: Cult Auteur 3
Stanley Kubrick: The Exhibition (*SK:TE*) 9–19
Stanley Kubrick: A Life in Pictures (*LiP*) (2001) 5, 88
Stanley Kubrick and Me: Thirty Years at His Side 2
Stanley Kubrick: New York Jewish Intellectual 59
Stanley Kubrick's Sound Odyssey 106
Stanley Kubrick traveling exhibition 1, 3–4, 7, 97

Index 115

Stark, G. 90
Star Wars (1977) 44, 45
Steeds, L. 10
St. Matthew Passion 47
Strangelove soda 69
Stranger's Kiss (1983) 5, 88, 98
"Strangers in the Night" 42
Strauss, J. 49
Strauss, R. 41, 70
Sugarland Express, The (1974) 46
Sundance Channel (US) 79

2 Fast 2 Furious (2003) 78
2001: A Space Odyssey (1968) 1, 3, 4, 5, 11, 13, 15, 18, 22, 29, 37, 62, 104n5, 107; 70mm print of 18, 19n2; in advertising 70–72, 74, 75, 77, 79; documentary 94; IMAX 4k 107; music in 37, 39, 41, 43–46, 49, 50; newsreel 94; pronunciation: 80–81
2001: A Space Odyssey: A Look Behind the Future 94
Tales From the Crypt 73
Tarantino, Q. 47
tea break (union mandated) 98
technê 56
television *see* advertising
"Thieving Magpie" 89
"think about the unthinkable" (Kahn) 26
Thompson, K. 56
"Timesteps" 42
Toccata 49
Toronto International Film Festival (TIFF) 4–5, 9
Torrance, D. (*The Shining*) 60, 73–74, 95
Torrance family 59, 96
Torrance, J. (*The Shining*) 12, 60, 72, 79
Torrance, W. (*The Shining*) 74–75
To the Wonder (2012) 49
Townshend, H. 49
toys 71; Kubrick brand (Japan) 69, 82n3
Traumnovelle 78
Tree of Life, The (2011) 48
tropes 4–5, 67

"Try a Little Tenderness" 41
Tucci, S. 5, 99
Tucker, T. 42
Turandot 47
Turgidson, General Buck (*Dr. Strangelove*) 24–26, 93
"Turn Off the Moon" 41
Two Mules for Sister Sara (1970) 47

Ulivieri, F. 2
United International Pictures 93
Universal Studios 80
University of the Arts London *see* Stanley Kubrick Archive (SKA)
Unsworth, G. 94

Van Houtte coffee 77
Vietnam War 76, 98
Vitali, L. (Lord Bullingdon) 2; as Kubrick's assistant 59, 60, 95, 98, 102

Walgreens 70
Wallach, E. 14
Walt Disney Concert Hall 107
War Horse 10
Warner Brothers 18, 89
Weidner, J. 55
"We'll Meet Again" 41
Wente, J. 11, 12, 17
"When Johnny Comes Marching Home" 41
Whitehead, C. 10
Williams, J. 44, 46
Willingham, C. 107
Wolf at the Door: Stanley Kubrick, History, and the Holocaust, The 59
Woods, T. 71

Yentob, A. 95
YouTube 4, 52, 56, 60

Zierra, T. 2
Zweig, S. 107